COFFEE CREATIONS

90
DELICIOUS
RECIPES
FOR THE
PERFECT CUP

CELESTE WONG

MITCHELL BEAZLEY

For Mum, Dad & Macchiato

First published in Great Britain in 2024
by Mitchell Beazley, an imprint of
Octopus Publishing Group Ltd
Carmelite House
50 Victoria Embankment
London EC4Y 0DZ
www.octopusbooks.co.uk

An Hachette UK Company
www.hachette.co.uk

Distributed in the US by
Hachette Book Group
1290 Avenue of the Americas
4th and 5th Floors, New York, NY 10104

Distributed in Canada by
Canadian Manda Group
664 Annette St., Toronto
Ontario, Canada M6S 2C8

ISBN 978-1-78472-961-5

A CIP catalogue record for this book is
available from the British Library.

Printed and bound in China.

10 9 8 7 6 5 4 3 2 1

Commissioning Editor: Jeannie Stanley
Editor: Scarlet Furness
Copy Editor: Jo Smith
Art Director & Designer: Yasia Williams
Photographers: Steve Ryan and Jake Green
Prop Stylist: Max Robinson
Food Stylist: Christina Mackenzie
Assistant Production Manager:
Allison Gonsalves

Standard level spoon measurements are used
in all recipes.
1 tablespoon = one 15ml spoon
1 teaspoon = one 5ml spoon

Both imperial and metric measurements have been
given in all recipes. Use one set of measurements
only and not a mixture of both.

Eggs should be medium unless otherwise stated.
The Department of Health advises that eggs should
not be consumed raw. This book contains dishes
made with raw or lightly cooked eggs. It is prudent
for more vulnerable people such as pregnant and
nursing mothers, the elderly, babies and young
children to avoid uncooked or lightly cooked dishes
made with eggs. Once prepared these dishes should
be kept refrigerated and used promptly.

Fresh herbs should be used unless otherwise
stated. If unavailable use dried herbs as an
alternative but halve the quantities stated.

Ovens should be preheated to the specific
temperature – if using a fan-assisted oven,
follow manufacturer's instructions for adjusting
the time and the temperature.

All microwave information is based on a 650 watt
oven. Follow manufacturer's instructions for an
oven with a different wattage.

This book includes dishes made with nuts and
nut derivatives. It is advisable for customers
with known allergic reactions to nuts and nut
derivatives and those who may be potentially
vulnerable to these allergies, such as babies
and children with a family history of allergies,
to avoid dishes made with nuts and nut oils. It
is also prudent to check the labels of pre-
prepared ingredients for the possible inclusion
of nut derivatives.

Contents

Introduction: coffee culture

When I first landed in London, the coffee scene was nearly non-existent. Monmouth Coffee in Borough Market was the lone ranger in the speciality coffee game, with other options sparse. Back in 2004, Aussie investor Peter Hall, fed up with London's lacklustre coffee, teamed up with New Zealanders James Gurnsey and Cameron McClure to birth Flat White on the lively Berwick Street in Soho. Picture this: a creative hub amid fruit stalls, food tents, second-hand shops and traditional pubs – and, oh, nestled in the red-light district. This place was the epicentre for film and fashion, an eclectic mix of people all craving a caffeine boost.

Even before my arrival, I'd heard whispers about Flat White in London. Luckily, they were expecting me, and a job offer quickly followed. I was extremely excited by their central location and stellar reputation. Little did I know, it was the go-to spot for any Antipodean soul in London because it was the 'only place to get a decent Flat White', which I heard on repeat. The word spread like wildfire. People on tight deadlines were hitting us up four times a day, blown away by our (looking back, ridiculously strong) coffee. I lost count of how many times I explained what a Flat White was. It was repetitive (we eventually wrote the definition on the wall behind us), but it was something special. The vibe, the curiosity from customers, it was all evolving right in front of us and, even if we weren't consciously aware, that

energy fuelled us. We knew we were making a positive impact on people's days, and to me, that's as crucial as the coffee itself. And in that vibrant corner of Soho, it was our reality. A special time and place that played a pivotal role in reshaping the landscape of the UK's burgeoning coffee industry.

In the UK, where the tea tradition runs deep from colonial history in India and a strong connection to the monarchy, the coffee industry faced an uphill battle. Yet, many years later, I'm chatting on America's most-watched daytime TV show *The Today Show* and the UK's favourite Saturday morning cooking show *Saturday Kitchen Live*. Why? Because coffee consumption has finally surpassed that of tea in the UK... a transition I'd always hoped for, but never expected to happen.

Needless to say, speciality coffee and coffee culture have evolved tremendously the world over from when I first experienced them in New Zealand, then witnessed what we call the 'third wave' of coffee in Melbourne, only to be a part of the evolution again in the UK years later. And even though coffee in Europe, the USA and Asia has always been hugely popular, coffee culture and the uptake of speciality coffee in particular has advanced substantially.

I hope this book will equip and inspire you to join the journey and take advantage of my knowledge and insight, to create your own coffee creations at home.

What is coffee?

The best thing in the world... and it originated in Ethiopia in the 15th century. No one really knows who discovered it or when, but the most commonly preferred story (and mine too) is about a couple of goats that were discovered dancing by their young shepherd. Thinking that his goats were possessed after he witnessed them biting leaves off a tree and chewing bright red cherries, he was scared they might die and that he would get in trouble with his father. Fortunately, they lived, and the next day while walking through the mountains with them, he saw the same thing happen. They ate leaves and berries off trees and they began to jump, dance and vocalize their existence!

The curious boy tried it for himself, and the legend goes that he started speaking poetry, singing songs, frolicking with his goats, and thought he'd never tire of it. After telling his father of this experience, word of mouth about this miracle berry tree spread.

Around the mid-15th century, Yemen was occupied by the Turks, so coffee exporting became a lucrative trade throughout the Turkish empire. To protect their product, they adhered to very strict rules that the beans were not allowed to germinate once they left the port. The coffee beans were therefore either partially boiled or roasted. This worked until the 1600s when a Muslim pilgrim named Baba Budan smuggled seven seeds into Southern India by taping them to his stomach. Through trade, coffee then reached the Arab states, where it was highly popular, initially used medicinally and to help the monks stay awake for prayer.

Coffee as we know it was successfully cultivated around the 1600s and soon spread to Holland and then all over the world. The wealthy started drinking it in their homes, and coffee houses started to pop up. However, coffee gained a rebellious reputation due to the 'trouble' it caused through the heightened energy in the people who drank it. Many coffee houses were shut down and then reopened around this time! Coffee has had a rollercoaster of a history due to the contradictory nature of its effects – caffeine has an

addictive quality, while also stimulating intellectual thought, which lead to lively and important conversations and connections in business and the arts.

Europeans were very passionate about coffee, and Italians started serving it on the streets on every corner. Coffee houses became synonymous with boosting social morale and were adopted in France and Britain. In Britain in the 17th century, they were often called Penny Universities because people of all walks of life, from politicians to artists, would pay a penny to enter. There they would drink the black stuff and learn about philosophy, art, science, politics and business through the conversations they had over coffee.

Not that much has changed today, except now cafés have also become safe havens for people to relax alone if they wish, to get lost in the sanctuary of their Mocha, Frappuccino or Long Black. One thing that has stayed true is that coffee itself and the industry is ever evolving.

From bean to cup

Coffee is a big wide world, and a large part of what keeps me interested is that it is constantly evolving. We might never know everything there is to know about coffee, but we can always start with the fundamentals.

Coffee beans

Good coffee starts with good-quality beans. For optimal freshness and flavour in your coffee, it's best to purchase and use whole coffee beans whenever possible – my go-to motto is 'fresh is always best'. Coffee, when in the form of whole beans, maintains its freshness for an extended period, contributing to an enhanced flavour experience. The moment green coffee beans undergo roasting, they

release carbon dioxide, influencing the overall taste profile. Over time, these beans undergo oxidation, leading to a gradual development of a 'stale' and flat taste. Grinding coffee exposes a larger surface area to oxygen, accelerating the loss of freshness. Therefore, it is better to keep coffee in its whole form until just before consumption.

If you can, buy fresh beans regularly instead of bulk buying. There are a number of coffee subscriptions available online so you can experiment with new flavours and have your favourite beans delivered to your door, even from your local café.

Types of coffee bean

Many people are surprised to find out that coffee is a fruit – the bean is actually a seed inside a juicy cherry growing on a branch of a coffee plant. There are over 120 species of coffee plant and, within that, many varieties. There are four main types of coffee bean: Arabica, Robusta, Liberica and Excelsa. The first two are probably the most familiar types because they are the most commonly produced coffee in the world, and together make up nearly 100 per cent of the market.

Arabica This is the most common type of coffee, accounting for over 60 per cent of output. It is considered the highest-quality coffee and produced by the speciality coffee industry. This variety is relatively hard to grow. Arabica beans have less caffeine than Robusta, but have more varied complex characteristics in taste and acidity levels because they are usually grown at higher altitudes, in better-quality, nutrient-rich soil. This is the kind of coffee you're most likely to buy and drink in a speciality coffee shop.

Robusta Robusta plants are hardy and the beans are usually used for commodity products like cheaper instant coffee. They are generally grown at a lower altitude and are higher in caffeine. If cultivated, processed and roasted expertly, the result can be quite pleasant. They would usually be used in a blend and have a slightly bolder, more homogenous flavour.

Liberica These almond-shaped beans are much bigger and more irregularly shaped than Robusta and Arabica beans and not commonly available. They have a smoky, floral and fruity flavour all at once.

Excelsa There is some ambiguity as to whether this plant belongs to the Liberica species, or whether it is its own species. Originating from Central Africa, it is now cultivated in Southeast Asia and India in small volumes. It's generally considered a lower-quality bean, but that might be to do with limited cultivation and processing knowledge. The beans are small and round and contain less caffeine than the others.

Coffee processing

There are now many different ways to process and ferment coffee, all of which have an effect on flavour and quality. Coffee, like wine, is a highly complex product, with quality greatly affected by environmental conditions and farming. Both also undergo fermentation, although any alcohol in the coffee fermentation process is taken out with the pulp. The processes are similar, except wine uses grapes and coffee uses the seeds within a coffee cherry, although sometimes the flesh of the cherry is used in processing to enhance and affect the flavour of the bean.

The age of vines significantly influences the quality of wine as older vines develop roots to access richer minerals, which enhance flavour concentration over time. Coffee trees, however, have a lifespan of only 20–30 years. Their most productive yield is in the earlier part of their life, between 7 and 20

years according to the National Coffee Association USA.

And of course, unlike wine, raw green coffee beans are heated and roasted to bring out the flavours. They have a much shorter shelf life due to the constant release of carbon dioxide after roasting, whereas wine can be left in a bottle to age for years to enhance flavour after processing. Both products are, however, tasted in very similar ways and can have very similar flavour profiles. We even have a coffee taster's flavour wheel similar to the wine taster's flavour wheel (see page 16 for a guide to flavour profiles and page 18 for a guide to cupping coffee).

Popular processes

Here are explanations of a few popular processes that you may see printed on packaging of good-quality coffee.

Washed coffee (wet processed) is often described as clean, clear or vibrant due to thorough cleaning of the beans before drying. This allows you to taste the coffee bean without the influence of other cherry components during processing. Fully washed coffee tends to have higher acidity, and be lighter in body and mouthfeel.

Natural (dry processed) is where the beans are left inside the whole cherries to be dried 'naturally' in the sunlight. Often my favourite, this process is known for producing more acidity, sweetness, fruity flavours and body and the resulting coffee is often described as 'funky'.

Semi-washed/Pulped natural (or honeyed processed) is a mixture of the above two methods, leaving some or all of the mucilage (the cherry pulp around the bean) during drying. While there are different levels of this process, it generally enhances sweetness in the coffee's taste profile.

Carbonic maceration As with wine, which has a longer history using this method, carbon dioxide is used to ferment the coffee cherries in a controlled environment. This softens the fruit and results in a sweet and fruity flavour profile with lower acidity and body.

Anaerobic fermentation involves depriving the coffee (whole cherries or beans) of oxygen in its fermentation process, producing distinct lactic acids that are constantly monitored and then further processed. It allows more control over the fermentation process, producing a more consistent flavour, often less bitter and creamier. Different temperatures used in this fermentation stage have been known to produce different characteristics too.

Aerobic fermentation is more straightforward, where fermentation is with naturally occurring oxygen. Coffee is de-pulped and washed, then left for 12–36 hours in tanks to let the yeast, oxygen and sugars react more naturally.

Yeast fermentation Yeast occurs naturally everywhere, so along with coffee's natural yeast enzymes, other strains of yeast are added to the tanks of green coffee beans soaking in water to enhance the quality of flavour.

Roasting revelations

Coffee roasting, alongside the growing, cultivating and processing, is one of the most important parts of the journey from farm to cup. Once the green beans are processed, they are ready to be browned. They are heated at high temperatures to develop flavour, aroma and colour. Coffee can be described as light, medium or dark.

Light-roasted coffee reaches the 'first crack' stage, exhibiting a warm, slightly browned colour. With no set flavour profile, this roast indicates shorter roasting time, allowing the dense green coffee bean flavours to shine. Light roasts often deliver more acidity and more complex flavours.

Medium-roasted coffee This goes a step further in the Maillard reaction (see page 31), offering a slightly darker version than the light roast. The extended time brings out more sweetness, maintaining some good acidity and complex flavours. A bolder or heavier mouthfeel can result from a longer roast, rounding out the overall flavour profile.

Dark-roasted coffee A dark roast pushes the coffee to its brink, hopefully before burning it! While some commercial roasters do still go too far, resulting in a bitter or burned taste, expertly roasted dark beans can achieve a bold, chocolatey and heavier flavour without crossing into unpleasant bitterness. Contrary to popular belief, darker roasts don't necessarily mean more caffeine: caffeine levels are more closely tied to the dry weight of the coffee used than the roast level and may vary depending on the coffee bean variety.

The perfect roast

Green coffee beans must be roasted expertly in order to emphasize and enhance their flavour characteristics. Too dark and they will taste bitter or burned, too light and they might taste acidic or grassy. As Goldilocks knew, there's often a sweet spot and the roaster must experiment with different coffee beans to reach that. But different beans coming from different origins that have been cultivated and processed in a variety of ways means there is no one 'recipe' or 'profile' (as we call it in the industry) for roasting. I've often marvelled at roasters who, like baristas after prolonged experience, develop an intuition that turns into some kind of mastery.

Roasters roast the beans to the 'first crack' – you can literally hear the beans making a cracking sound. This is the most common point to which speciality coffee gets taken. Coffees that go to the 'second crack' are usually lower-quality, commercial coffees (often Robusta), which are roasted to a much darker colour.

I often use the analogy of roasting meat to explain the nuances of coffee bean roasting. Imagine having three identical cuts of beef to roast. If you use a high temperature initially and then lower it for the first, roast the second at a low

temperature over a long time, and start the third at a low temperature but then blast it on high, each cut will turn out differently. Similarly, roasting coffee beans involves adjusting roast profiles to achieve the optimal flavour for that particular bean. Just as different meat-roasting methods yield varied results, tweaking the roast profile influences the taste and characteristics of the coffee beans.

Roasting is key to unveiling region-specific nuances, shaping distinct flavour profiles in beans from different countries. However, traditional characteristics associated with each coffee origin no longer strictly define its flavour today. Advancements and experimentation in growing, processing and roasting have led to a more diverse coffee experience.

Storing coffee

Coffee beans and ground coffee should be stored in a dark, dry environment. Keep them in an airtight container or in the original bag to limit the entry of oxygen and moisture. Coffee packaging often has a carbon dioxide release valve and there are also fit-for-purpose containers you can buy, which provide a vacuum canister.

To freeze or not to freeze?

In general, I wouldn't encourage freezing coffee, but freezers are designed to prevent oxidation so if you find you've bought more coffee than you can use in the next few weeks, you can freeze it. Technically, roasted coffee has very little water content so the flavour will still be preserved. Portion your coffee beans into 250g (9oz) portions (or however much you use per week) before freezing. It can be stored in reusable airtight containers such as freezer-proof jars or food bags (vacuum sealing is best, but has wasteful packaging). If you have enough space, you could portion out exactly what you brew each day.

At the start of the week, take the jar out of the freezer and leave it overnight to defrost. Don't open the lid until the next day when it has returned to room temperature as it will introduce oxygen and condensation will form, which is not good for the beans. Grind and use as soon as possible. Generally, it's better to try and buy only enough for one to three weeks at a time – fresh is always best!

Grinding coffee

Pairing top-notch coffee with an exceptional grinder can revolutionize your home-brewing experience, enhancing both the flavour and quality of your cup. A reliable grinder not only maximizes your coffee's potential but should also be practical, user-friendly, easy to clean and aesthetically pleasing. For optimal coffee results, look for grinders that deliver consistent grinds and cater to various brewing styles.

Amid the array of coffee grinders available, the main choice is between electric and manual. Both types can be either blade or burr operated.

Blade grinders, while more budget friendly and able to do the trick, tend to chop coffee unevenly, affecting extraction, and therefore taste. I also find them a bit messy. On the other hand, burr grinders with flat or conical burrs ensure more consistent grinds. Flat burrs, prevalent in commercial grinders, provide precision but may generate heat. Conical burrs consist of two cone-shaped burrs stacked to grind coffee, utilizing gravity and grinding more quietly. They are generally a little cheaper though slightly less consistent over a high volume. In domestic grinders, ceramic burrs offer heat resistance and durability, while steel burrs, known for sharpness, offer consistent initial grinds.

Grind guide for different brew methods

GRIND	DESCRIPTION	BREW METHOD
① Extra fine	The consistency of cocoa powder or cornflour	Turkish
② Fine	Finer than table salt, like fine sand	Espresso or moka pot
③ Fine to medium	A similar consistency to table salt	AeroPress, manual pourover cone including V60 and moka pot
④ Medium	The consistency of normal sand	Pourover cone, siphon, automatic drip coffeemakers and Chemex
⑤ Coarse	The consistency of sea salt	French press or cold brew
⑥ Extra coarse	The texture of peppercorns	Long cold-brew steeping

①   ②   ③

④   ⑤   ⑥

Exploring coffee origins: how to choos

There is such a wide world to explore within speciality coffee and its evolving flavours. In the supermarket, you might find an 'Italian blend' or labels like 'Kenyan' or 'Colombian'. Good packaging and transparent companies might offer more description on the bag, such as:

Strength: How strong it tastes

Roast: Medium, light or dark

Descriptors: Acidity, sweetness, body and so on

Tasting notes: Berry, nutty, dark chocolate…

I often suggest that people start by considering their favourite flavour profile first – just like with wine, there are many. Here I have broken them down into three easily identifiable flavour profiles:

Chocolate and nuts: Deep and bold

Fruity and floral: Berries and red fruits

Citrus and floral: Orange, zesty, pineapple, lemon

Chocolate and nuts

Coffees with this flavour profile are generally well balanced and full bodied with low acidity. They are rich and sometimes have hints of more rounded fruit, such as plums and darker berries.

Some countries typical of this flavour profile: Brazil, Guatemala, Nicaragua, Sumatra (Indonesia) and Mexico.

Fruity and floral

Generally, these can have wine-like qualities in mouthfeel; they are a little more elegant and complex, with a brighter, clean finish. The floral part of this profile usually comes through as a jasmine flower, honeysuckle, orange blossom or a similarly soft flower.

Some countries typical of this flavour profile: Ethiopia, Burundi, Tanzania, Rwanda, Honduras and Peru.

Citrus and floral

This flavour profile is generally quite balanced, with bright acidity. It is vibrant and might have hints of berry fruits too, and floral notes as above.

Some countries typical of this flavour profile: Colombia, Costa Rica, Kenya, Panama and El Salvador.

Speak up

People often confide in me about their coffee experiences. I once met someone who told me he didn't enjoy the coffee recommended by his favourite coffee shop, ground specifically for his moka pot. But he didn't provide feedback. I encouraged him to speak up! Sharing feedback is invaluable because coffee preferences are subjective, and for baristas, calibrating to diverse palates requires some trial and error. Let's assist cafés in finding the perfect match for you.

Coffee preferences are as unique as food tastes; everyone has a degree of sweetness or saltiness they enjoy. A knowledgeable barista can customize recommendations to suit individual palates. But it's a fun practice for you to notice and try to articulate what you are tasting and why. Keep in mind also that brewing methods and recipes play a role in flavour. If your coffee brew method misses the mark, try experimenting with espresso or try different filter roasts to unlock more desired flavours. There could be delightful surprises, which might help you choose better coffee for yourself. With a bit of exploration at home, you'll be a pro in no time.

I encourage you to develop your own personal taste preferences. Visit a local café and experiment, tasting different kinds of coffee and looking at the tasting notes on the bag to see if they match the flavours you pick up, while noting what appeals to your taste buds. Otherwise try your local supermarket or look online for independent coffee roasters in your area and see what is best for you at home, depending on how you brew and drink your coffee. Different coffees can lend themselves better to different brew methods.

Cupping & tasting

After coffee is roasted, speciality roasters typically engage in a coffee-tasting practice known as cupping, reminiscent of wine tasting. This official process involves evaluating numerous freshly roasted coffees simultaneously, often 6–24 cups at a time, and even up to 100 in certain settings (for example, when officially grading coffee at origin for market). The Specialty Coffee Association (SCA) sets the standard for cupping, specifying 8.25g (scant ¼oz) of whole beans, roasted within the last 24 hours, to be ground and mixed with 150ml (5fl oz) of hot water of approximately 93°C (200°F), adhering to a ratio of 55g (2oz) of coffee to 1 litre (1¾ pints) of water.

The cupping process follows a systematic evaluation using an official coffee-tasting score sheet for efficiency and consistency. However, many roasters make their own: they generally note characteristics such as roast colour, aroma at various stages, clarity of the cup, defects, sweetness, acidity (as with wine, this can be a good thing), mouthfeel, flavour, aftertaste, balance and overall comments. The tasting ritual involves smelling the aroma of the coffee before and after adding hot water and letting the coffee brew for four minutes. After breaking the crust that forms on the surface, tasters quickly note the wet coffee aroma and remove the grounds.

When it comes to tasting, the slurping technique is essential. Tasters use a specially designed cupping spoon, making a loud, whistle-like noise while slurping to coat their entire mouths and taste buds. Between each taste, they rinse their spoons in hot water, tapping off the excess liquid. For those evaluating numerous coffees, spitting out the coffee into a spittoon, similar to that used in wine tasting, is a common practice. The rigorous process allows roasters to efficiently assess and score various coffees in a short time span. In coffee tasting and making, it helps to engage all your senses (sight, smell, touch, sound and taste) to enhance the experience.

Try this at home

I find it quite difficult to test more than 12–15 different coffees at a time at most, because it can get quite overwhelming. But it's a fun way to try a few different coffees at home. You can really note the difference when you are tasting coffees that have been prepared in exactly the same way, trying one after the other. Describing and discussing flavours with others can also really help too. So please give this a go home. Get 2–6 different coffees, grind the same amount into identical cups or glasses following my description above. Add water just off the boil (93–96°C/199–205°F – you can achieve this by leaving the boiled kettle lid open for 30 seconds before pouring), then slurp the coffee in each cup. Sometimes it helps to eat a plain biscuit or cracker in between coffees to reset your palate.

Brewing

Increasing numbers of brew methods are being created, but the main two are espresso and different iterations of filter coffee.

Espresso Espresso machines are classed as anything that yields concentrated coffee using high pressure and hot water up to 96°C (205°F). This technique usually uses single origin coffees or blends that might be roasted slightly darker. The ratio for espresso is typically 1:2 coffee to water. The coffee from stovetop moka pots (see page 22) is not technically espresso, neither is that from pod machines in my book, but they do have similar qualities. The main difference is that the amount of coffee used in a pod is substantially lower: only 5–7g (about ⅛oz) per 30ml (1fl oz) shot, versus 15–20g (½–¾oz) in a more robust traditional espresso machine. But the flavour can still be adequate, depending on the pod brand and machine type.

When brewing espresso to be served with milk, the espresso needs to be heavy and bold, and balanced so that the flavour can cut through the milk. Coffee that is too lightly roasted or high in acidity can taste sour with milk.

For more on espresso, see page 35.

Filter coffees Filter coffees are known for highlighting specific flavour characteristics and are wonderful! Typically, they undergo a lighter roast compared to espresso roast, although some are omni-roasted to accommodate both preferences of espresso and filter.

Opting for filter coffee often allows you to discern more nuanced and distinct flavours, providing a richer-tasting experience compared to other brewing methods.

As a general rule for medium-strength coffee, use a ratio of 1:16 coffee to water, for example 25g (1oz) of coffee with 400ml (14fl oz) of water, or 100g (3½oz) with 1.6 litres (2¾ pints) if making a bigger batch. Keeping this ratio in mind is helpful if you're at the end of a bag of coffee and are wondering how much water to brew it with. Say you have 20g (¾oz) of coffee left – multiply this by 16 to get your water amount: 320ml (11fl oz). If you prefer your coffee stronger, you can decrease the ratio of water to coffee. Likewise, if you prefer your coffee a bit weaker, you can increase the water ratio.

Water Before we get into the brew methods, the importance of water is not to be overlooked. After coffee itself, water is the next most important ingredient that will affect how your coffee tastes. Good quality water is recommended, and I suggest using filtered water if you can. According to the SCA, a pH value of 6.5 to 7.5 is optimal. Installing a water softener could help in areas with hard water. I would recommend using filtered water in your appliances too, for their longevity.

On the following pages are four really easy but satisfying brew methods with recipe instructions you can do at home.

Cafetière

Also known as a French press, plunger coffee maker, cafetière *à piston*, *caffettiera a stantuffo*, press pot or coffee press. It is made up of a jug-like base with a lid, a plunger, a spiral plate with a filter and a cross plate and is commonly made from glass, plastic, metal or ceramic. It's important that the metal filter aligns with the walls of the jug to prevent coffee grounds from getting in the cup. It's no-mess, no-fuss brewing, in either small or large volumes, so useful for when you want to make more than one cup. This recipe makes 300ml (10fl oz) to serve one.

EQUIPMENT

- Scales (optional)
- Cafetière

INGREDIENTS

- 20g (³⁄₄oz) medium- to coarse-ground coffee
- 300ml (10fl oz) hot water

Place the coffee in the cafetière, followed by the hot water just off the boil and stir. Place the lid on with the mesh filter sitting above the surface of the coffee but not touching it.

Leave to brew for 3-4 minutes. The coffee will settle to the bottom of the cafetière. Slowly press the mesh filter down through the liquid. Pour immediately for a hot cup.

Double or triple this recipe for larger volumes. Remember, it is better to make a stronger brew and add hot water to dilute it afterwards than to make a brew too weak.

Moka pot

Moka pots or stovetop coffeemakers are among the most common and preferred ways to make coffee in Europe. They make very strong coffee, and are often mistakenly interchanged with espresso, although coffee from a moka pot is not as concentrated as an espresso. By heating the water in its base, the moka pot creates steam and pressure and pushes the water vapour up through the coffee into a chamber above that collects it. There are many different versions, depending on what kind of stove you have (electric, gas or induction). This recipe makes 60-100ml (2¼-3½fl oz) to serve two to three.

EQUIPMENT

- 2-cup moka pot
- Scales (optional)

INGREDIENTS

- 15g (½oz) fine-ground coffee
- 60-100ml (2¼-3½fl oz) water

Fill the moka pot base with cold water up to the pressure valve, but not over it. Place about 15g (½oz) of ground coffee in the perforated basket or to the top until level without tamping it down. Screw the chamber on top.

Place the moka pot on the stove and heat. As the water boils, it will create pressure and push the liquid coffee up into the chamber. Be careful, it's hot!

You can check that the coffee has started to percolate by opening the lid. But be careful, it can be hot to touch!

AeroPress

The AeroPress is my go-to for its speed, simplicity, ease of cleaning and delightful taste. It's also compact and light, which is great when travelling. This foolproof method, which uses air pressure to extract flavours, is suitable for most coffees. With a filter at the base, the coffee often has a fuller mouthfeel compared to the delicate taste of that from a pourover. While some opt for a stronger AeroPress by increasing the ratio of coffee to water, this recipe aligns more with the strength of coffee from a pourover cone, resembling a filter coffee. This recipe makes 250ml (9fl oz) to serve one.

EQUIPMENT

- **AeroPress filter papers or reusable metal filter**
- **AeroPress**
- **Stirrer or spoon** (one comes with the AeroPress)
- **Cup or jug to catch the coffee**

INGREDIENTS

- **15–20g (½–¾oz) medium-ground coffee**
- **250ml (9fl oz) hot water**

Position the paper filter in the screen and attach to the base of the AeroPress. Use 2 or 3 filters for a cleaner brew, but it will create slightly more resistance when pressing.

Tip your ground coffee into the AeroPress using the funnel provided in the kit. Now add hot water just off the boil (93–96°C/199–205°F) up to the first number on the tube. It will 'bloom' for a few seconds, which is when the coffee and water first mix, and it releases gases, 'blooms' up and bubbles. It generally happens much more vividly when coffee is fresh.

Stir it lightly with a spoon or spatula. You are agitating the coffee grounds here to make sure that they are evenly saturated.

Continue to pour in water slowly until you almost reach the maximum level of the AeroPress (approximately 250ml/9fl oz). Place the rubber part inside the top, making sure it is sealed. Wait for about 1½ minutes.

Using the palm of your hand, press down gently on the top to release the coffee – the resistance should feel even. Stop just when it starts to 'wheeze' or 'fizz'. Discard the used coffee by unscrewing the perforated screen and pushing the coffee 'puck' out.

Pourover cone

This is probably my favourite way to filter coffee. Not only for the ritual of it, but it gives a clean, flavourful cup. You can really taste the nuances of coffee using this method. I suggest using a gooseneck kettle, which is a kettle with a long, curved spout. It is safer as you can control the flow more easily than with a regular kitchen kettle. Gooseneck kettles come in both electric and stovetop options and are great for camping too. There are some more expensive temperature-controlled gooseneck kettles but also some good options at the lower price range. This recipe makes 500ml (18fl oz) to serve two.

EQUIPMENT

- Pourover cone
- Jug
- Paper coffee filter
- Scales (optional)
- Watch or timer

INGREDIENTS

- 35–40g (1¼–1½oz) medium-ground coffee
- 500ml (18fl oz) hot water

Put the cone over a jug and line the cup with a paper filter. Pour hot water over the filter until saturated to rinse it thoroughly (to eliminate any paper taste). Pour the excess water out of the jug and discard.

Place the coffee into the filter. Using water just off the boil, slowly start to pour in a circular motion into the bed of coffee until the grounds are saturated. Start your timer for 3 minutes.

The grounds will bloom and bubble and give a lovely aroma. You can give them a short gentle stir here to make sure all the coffee grounds are wet, and then carry on with your slow pour.

Over the next 3 minutes, very slowly pour the water into and over the coffee, trying not to let it 'drop'. The trick is to pour slowly in a circular motion for 10–20 seconds, then stop, then pour again for 10–20 seconds. Repeat this until you have reached your target water volume. Pouring in a circular motion helps the even distribution of water and extraction.

When your 3 minutes is almost over you should be near the target volume of coffee. How much water you have left at this point is how you can tell if your coffee is ground to the right size. If you still have lots of water left to add, the coffee grind may be too fine. If you run out of water well before 3 minutes is up, the coffee may be too coarse.

Competition

Back on the vibrant streets of Melbourne, where the third wave of coffee was just starting to ripple, I found myself managing Batch Espresso, a small New Zealand-themed haven in St Kilda East where Jason Chan, a mentor and undiscovered genius, then led the charge. At this time, a sudden surge of new competitors, including the global giant Starbucks, was emerging.

I recall asking Jason with a touch of apprehension about his thoughts on the influx of competitors. His response was a lesson in resilience and foresight. 'Competition,' he said, looking out at the bustling street, 'is a driving force for quality. More people mean more scrutiny, and that pushes us to be better, which is better for everyone.' His words resonated with me and left an indelible mark on my perspective.

Melbourne's discerning coffee enthusiasts proved that authenticity and individuality held significant power, causing Starbucks to depart the Melbourne coffee scene almost as quickly as it had entered. The narrative shifted from anxiety to empowerment, emphasizing the importance of owning and honing our craftmanship and uniqueness. This transformative time influenced not only Melbourne's coffee culture, but served as an encouraging example for other markets and became a chapter in my personal story of growth. A showcase of the impact a community can make.

In a parallel journey, my perspective on coffee competitions evolved. Once skeptical, I now appreciate events like The World Barista Championship, World Brewers Cup (both founded by the SCA) and the Coffee Masters championship and their comprehensive criteria for evaluating baristas. These competitions also become a spectator sport, foster learning and add vibrancy to the coffee industry, aligning the essence of our passionate community.

Having managed highly regarded cafés, I've witnessed the impact of baristas and competitions first hand. Figures like James Hoffman and Maxwell Colonna-Smalls demonstrate how competitions can open doors to success in various ventures. Yet, every barista, whether on stage or behind the counter contributes uniquely to our vibrant industry and people's daily lives. It's a reminder that competition, whether professionally or just with ourselves, enriches our journey as much as the brews we create.

Latte art: steaming milk

When I first started making coffee many many years ago, my coffee mentor was creating perfect double rosettas in his milk a long time before Latte art was seen anywhere else. As a baby barista, I worked tirelessly to transform the blob on top of the coffee to a smooth and creamy thing of beauty, almost too good to drink. Temperature, technique and a basic understanding of the science behind the components of milk and heating will help get your milk texture just right, so you can create your own masterpieces at home.

Milk is made up of fat, protein and carbohydrate (lactose). When heated, the fatty acids begin to stabilize and produce the 'foam'. Despite the common belief that low-fat milk is easier to foam, I disagree. Although it may seem more manageable, it tends to result in a thinner and less viscous mouthfeel. Higher fat content leads to improved stability, meaning the foam holds better. I would also encourage, where possible, cafés and homes around the world to purchase milk produced by farms committed to ethical, sustainable practices. Brades Farm Dairy in Lancashire, England, crafts milk specifically for coffee, blending Jersey and Holstein cows' milk for an ideal fat-to-protein ratio, ensuring the perfect milk for Latte art. Having been lucky enough to visit the farm, I've observed their ground-breaking and innovative approach to dairy farming first hand (and seen it featured in the *New York Times*). The cows are very happy and friendly!

With the array of milk alternatives, the same science applies. You may have noticed 'Barista' versions of oat or coconut milk – generally it means more oils have been added to ensure it steams with a nice texture. Feel free to use your preferred milk or plant-based alternative whenever I mention 'milk' in this book.

Steaming milk with a steam wand creates microbubbles, forming a dense milk foam. Too much air creates larger, weaker bubbles, reminiscent of old-style cappuccinos with cold, airy foam lacking texture. You can only really draw good Latte art with smoothly textured milk, not with bubbly, rigid milk. Whichever method you use, one way to get a silky smooth (almost marshmallow-like) finish is to tap the jug against a surface after heating to disperse any large air bubbles, and swirl.

Using a steam wand or wand attachments

- Always start with cold milk rather than warmed milk. If you're using leftover warmed milk, cool it down with some cold milk.

- When steaming milk, aim for a swirling, whirlpool motion in your jug.

- Make sure the wand is below the surface of the milk to avoid introducing cold air that will make it weak and bubbly. An awful loud hissing sound is an obvious indicator this is happening.

- If you do get a few bubbles, cover the jug with one hand, then gently bang the jug on the counter to pop weak bubbles. Then try swirling the milk a few times in the jug to get it silkier and smoother.

- Make sure you have good strong pressured steam injecting the milk to push and heat the milk adequately.

- 'Stretching' milk refers to the expansion of the milk foam. Generally, placing the tip of the wand closer to the surface creates thicker milk. The further down into the jug the wand is, the faster the milk will be heated and less foam texture will be created.

- Be mindful not to overheat the milk. There is an intersection where heat optimizes the sugars and fat in the milk. When you go beyond this point, milk can taste a little lacklustre, thin and less sweet. The ideal temperature of milk for coffee is about 65-67°C (149-153°F). Some people like to use a temperature gauge, which can help – it's easy to find one online that fixes to your milk jug.

To achieve:
Thick and creamy ① Position the steam wand just underneath the surface of the milk. This is also known as 'Cappuccino milk'.

Smooth and creamy milk ② Position the wand under the surface about two-thirds of the way down. This is also known as 'Latte milk'.

Hot, 'wet' milk, with thinner, 'flatter' foam ③ Position the wand nearer to (but not touching) the base of the jug. This position also heats the milk much faster, so keep an eye on the temperature. This is also known as 'Flat White milk'.

Alternative options

These are a couple of lo-tech ways to heat and foam milk. The microbubbles (foam) won't be as firm as other more efficient methods but it will provide you with some nice texture.

- Heat the milk in a saucepan or microwave, then use a small battery-operated milk 'whiz' to aerate it. This method can be done with cold milk too.

- Another way is to put milk heated on the stove or in the microwave into a French press and use the press to aerate the milk, pulling the filter plunger up and down and pushing the milk through the mesh filter over and over to aerate it. This method can be done with cold milk too.

Basic shapes

Latte art is fun, so start with the basics – apples and hearts. Hold the jug near the centre of the cup of espresso coffee. Push the jug tip down, lifting the base upwards. Observe how the heavier 'wet' milk stays at the bottom while the frothy milk cascades over the top. Practise one slow and one fast pour without any unnecessary movements to note the difference. Once you understand how these form, your progression to rosettas or tulips will be seamless.

In a café setting, Latte art is a good indication that the barista is practised and has trained hard to control that aspect of coffee making, time and time again. But it isn't the pinnacle of a good coffee. Espresso quality is the main contributor to a tasty, well-made coffee.

Coffee curation

Most recipes in this book align with typical café serving sizes, ranging from 125–350ml (4–12fl oz). While you're creating your home café, feel free to customize, but a standard glass or cup size of 225–350ml (8–12fl oz) is recommended.

Garnishes

A garnish can be, quite literally, the cherry on top that sometimes completes the serve. Some drinks are better off minimalistic, while others are elevated by their garnishes. They are not only there for aesthetic pleasure, but also for aromatics and flavour. Where appropriate, I have made some simple suggestions for garnishes on each serve, but they are in no way exhaustive. Feel free to make use of any fresh herbs or odd pieces of fruit at home that you think might work. After all, garnishing drinks and food can be half the fun, so get creative and feel free to play.

Some classic garnishes

Lemon or lime wedges, peel or zest; hot chocolate powder; ground cinnamon or grated nutmeg; maraschino cherries (though I prefer a fresh cherry where possible); herbs such as mint, basil leaves or rosemary; whipped cream.

Some other fun suggestions

Cucumber ribbons; grated chocolate; red chilli pepper; edible flowers; lemon peel twist; M&Ms or your favourite sweets; cookies or biscuits; honey; cardamom or ground ginger.

What coffee to use in cocktails?

If you are going for a more subtle, refined coffee flavour in a cocktail, use a cold brew (see page 67) or filter, or an espresso made from a light- to medium-roast coffee. Use fresh coffee where possible rather than instant. If you are looking for a bolder, heavier flavour where coffee is the hero – like in an Espresso Martini – it's good to use a darker-roast espresso. Espresso is generally punchier because it is concentrated.

What coffee to use with milk?

Opting for a medium or dark roast is key, so it can cut through the milk. A slightly darker roast, with nutty and chocolatey undertones, tends to complement milk well. Lighter roasts, while boasting acidity that can be appreciated in certain instances, might not always work as smoothly when mixed with milk. Flavour is also influenced by the origin and quality of the beans. Espresso beans are often crafted as blends and showcase a balanced base flavour (such as Brazilian beans), with smaller percentages of other origins and types of coffee to contribute different flavour profiles such as fruity or floral notes. A good espresso blend won't taste overpowering but will hopefully create an intriguing profile that works harmoniously as both espresso and with added milk.

When to use instant coffee?

Instant coffee is dried-out coffee extract, which can be instantly redissolved in hot water. So in baking, instant coffee shines with its intense flavour, easy measurement and solubility, avoiding grit and excess liquid. However, not all instants are made the same! Speciality brands are innovating with flavour and focusing on bean quality and processing. Opt for natural coffee extracts over synthetic or artificial ones. Freeze-dried instant coffee produces better flavour and aroma than spray-dried versions, which can taste burned. Instant coffee can use Arabica or Robusta beans, with Arabica generally being higher quality and better tasting. Nutritionally, instant coffee generally has less caffeine (due to the drying process) than traditionally made fresh coffee, but luckily it still includes a lot of coffee's antioxidants, which is great. While most instant coffees work well in recipes, quality matters. Coffee extracts (derived from coffee beans) offer a concentrated flavour (see page 185).

Please know that whatever the type of coffee I suggest using in the recipes that follow, you can use whichever form you have access to at home. An espresso can be most closely substituted for moka pot or pod coffee, or perhaps even a very concentrated AeroPress – the flavour will vary, but that's exciting! Where cold brew or concentrated cold brew is recommended, cooled filter coffee can be used instead.

Using coffee in baking

This is where it gets tricky. Coffee, like salt, is a brilliant ingredient, subtly enhancing flavours. It's really quite exciting to think what dishes we can add coffee to – both sweet and savoury. But making coffee the star, for example in a coffee cake or cookies, blurs the lines. In general, expect subtler coffee flavours than the hit you'd get from your first sip in the morning. One thing that might affect this is the Maillard reaction, a chemical reaction that happens between sugar and protein (amino acids) when heated. It happens when coffee is roasted or when anything is baked at a certain temperature. We can get caramelization and browning. Because the raw, robust coffee aroma seems to weaken when baked (again) or heated while blending with added sugars, the Maillard reaction may affect the intensity or perhaps our perception of the coffee flavours. To keep the bold coffee taste, I've experimented in my recipes, offering flexibility to adjust the intensity, especially through additions like icing (which don't get baked). In my daily cooking, where possible, I add a teaspoon of fresh fine-ground coffee into blended soups or hearty stews, similar to salt. It doesn't taste like coffee, it gets absorbed and gives some depth to the dish.

**Classic café brews to start
your day the best way.**

Good
Mornings

1

Espresso

Also referred to as a 'short black', espresso is the base of many coffee drinks. It is a strong concentrated extraction of brewed coffee. Espresso uses finely ground coffee beans to maximize the surface area of the granules, making the coffee highly soluble in water – the secret to rapid brewing. It is brewed at a high temperature, using an espresso machine. The magic of high pressure enables a rich and robust flavour. The degree of intensity and quality depends on your espresso machine and the type of coffee beans and roast you use.

Generally, a single shot of espresso uses 7–8g (about ⅛oz) of ground coffee to extract about 30ml (1fl oz) of liquid coffee, while a double shot will use 15–20g (½–¾oz) of coffee to extract 30–50ml (1–2fl oz) of liquid coffee. This recipe is for a double espresso.

INGREDIENTS
- 15–20g (½–¾oz) fine-ground coffee

METHOD
Grind the beans and fill the basket. Press down or 'tamp' firmly with a tamper. Insert the portafilter firmly into the machine and start the water flow. It should take 30–45 seconds to extract 30–50ml (1–2fl oz) of concentrated espresso.

Ristretto

A ristretto is a 'restricted' espresso. It is the liquid resulting from the first 10–20 seconds of extraction of the espresso, stopped a little short. It is the thicker, sweetest part of the espresso, with all the intensity but half the volume.

Tips for good espresso

- Where possible, use good-quality speciality coffee beans.
- Grind your beans finely, like fine sand rather than a powder.
- Tamp firmly to ensure there are no gaps or 'channels' in the coffee for the hot water to run through. If water runs through these gaps instead of being absorbed and pushed through the coffee granules themselves, it will result in an uneven extraction – you may end up with light-coloured, watery espresso running out of your spouts very quickly, or it might spray out in different directions.
- Your espresso should look dark and thick in consistency. Aim for the liquid to trail down into the cup slowly at first, thick at the top and tapering down like a mouse's tail.
- Espresso should extract at an even speed – not too fast, not too slow. It will be slower at the beginning, then it will speed up as resistance lessens.
- When your espresso starts to look thinner and more watery – and becomes a lighter brown-yellow ('blonde') or starts to 'pulse' or waver – wait one or two seconds from this point, then switch the water flow off.

Macchiato

A Macchiato is a double espresso with a spot of heated textured milk. The name means 'stain' – you are staining your coffee with milk, so it should really only be a small amount of frothy milk on top of the espresso to take the 'edge' off it. If you're making a Flat White at the same time, it's more economical to use some of that milk, so you are not heating and wasting too much milk. Personally, I like to drink my Macchiatos from a small ceramic cup so that I can smell the aroma and feel the texture of the coffee as well as, of course, tasting it. But it also looks great presented in a small glass. It always reminds me of my favourite pet of all time, an all-black tuxedo cat with a tiny bit of milk on his chin – called, of course, Macchiato.

INGREDIENTS

- 1 double shot of espresso
- Heated textured milk

METHOD

Extract the espresso into an espresso cup or glass.

Steam the milk. If you are using an espresso machine steam wand, hold the wand at least 1–2cm (½–¾ inch) under the surface of the milk, making sure you don't let any cold air in. It shouldn't make any hissing noises or spit milk drops anywhere. Try to use the steam jets to spin the milk around in a whirlpool-like motion.

If you have a separate steamer attachment on your bean-to-cup machine, you might want to steam the milk separately in a jug so you can pour it yourself. (See pages 26–9 for more on steaming milk.)

Carefully pour a drop (I mean it, just a drop) of milk into the espresso and scoop about 1 heaped teaspoon of warm frothed milk over the top.

Cappuccino

In the early days of my barista journey, crafting the perfect cup of coffee consumed my world. Espresso and milk texture became my daily pursuits. I meticulously emulated my bosses' techniques, honing my skills until every pour was a dance of consistency. The daily 2pm Cappuccino milk texture tests were nerve-wracking but served as my proving ground.

Beyond merely pleasing the bosses or enhancing the business, this strive for excellence was about personal growth. It was about proving that I could stick with something, become truly skilled, be curious about my new passion and cultivate a profound ability to focus.

In my opinion, the 'traditional Cappuccino' might be the most difficult coffee to get right. The milk needs to be heated and textured perfectly to get that layered effect. Historically, the drink takes its name from the Capuchin friars – the colour of the espresso mixed with frothed milk was reminiscent of the colour of their robes. It is also said to symbolize the Italian flag, which makes sense as I have always made the Cappuccino with one-third espresso, one-third heated milk, topped with one-third creamy, textured milk. The trick is to float the perfectly foamed milk delicately on top of a well-extracted espresso, so that the wet milk dissipates and doesn't fully mix through the espresso. The foam should settle lightly on top of the creamy wetter milk so the drink in its entirety is still at a hot temperature. The foam is still warm, and when the Cappuccino is tilted to your lips, it glides into your mouth in such a way that you can taste and feel each layer separately and get a flavourful hit of espresso at the end! It is the most incredible drink if done this way. Often the milk is dusted with cocoa, chocolate or ground cinnamon.

A well-made, 'proper' Cappuccino is hard to come by. You might just make a better Cappuccino at home yourself... just saying. Goodbye 1980s retro, cold bubbly foam dumped on top of your coffee! This is a delicious, strong coffee and goes perfectly with a cookie.

INGREDIENTS

- 1 double shot of espresso
- 225–250ml (8–9fl oz) heated textured milk

METHOD

Extract the espresso into a 225–300ml (8–10fl oz) cup.

Heat and stretch your milk (see pages 26–9 for a detailed explanation). Gently layer the heated textured milk on top of the espresso until the milk reaches the top of the cup. If using a milk pouring jug, hold the base of it up to encourage the thicker foamy milk to glide out. Don't be afraid to add a little more milk to the cup to get that slightly raised dome on top of the coffee.

Latte

INGREDIENTS

- 1 double shot of espresso
- 300ml (10fl oz) heated textured milk

METHOD

Extract the espresso into a 350ml (12fl oz) cup. Heat your milk (see pages 26–9).

Gently layer the heated textured milk on top of the espresso until the milk reaches the top. If using a milk pouring jug, hold the base of it up to encourage the thicker foamy milk to glide out. The frothy head of milk should be about 1.5cm (5⁄8 inch) deep.

If you order a 'latte' in Italy, don't be shocked if you get just a glass of milk because that's what the name means. Ask instead for a 'caffè latte', which consists of steamed milk without foam and a single espresso.

The Latte, as we know it in most places that have adopted it, is generally one or two shots of espresso, depending on who's making it, with lots of heated milk. It's rare to find Latte bowls these days but maybe they'll make a renaissance. Over the years in the speciality coffee industry, vessel sizes have got smaller. But let's not go too wild! A Latte should be larger and therefore require more milk than a Flat White (see page 125), and taste weaker from the dilution from the milk. The frothy head of a Latte should be almost double that of a creamy, well-made Flat White. The texture is still smooth, but more full and slightly more airy or thicker than a Flat White. Syrups can offer a wide variety of flavours, from pumpkin, caramel and nuts to fruit. You can add almost any syrup to your Latte to flavour it differently.

In my first café job, unwavering simplicity was key. We offered only full-fat milk and a high-quality soy option, Bonsoy, from Japan. I vividly recall a lady giving the owner an earful for not having semi-skimmed milk. Despite that, I always appreciated how they kept things straightforward and efficient. It is amusing to reflect on those days, considering the plethora of alternative plant-based milk options that are considered a must-have now! As the climate crisis increasingly threatens, finding innovative and better ways to craft these small indulgences so that people can have variety and choice is both encouraging and necessary.

Cortado

This is a version of the Flat White (see page 125) that originates in Spain. It's a short, milky coffee made with espresso and 'cut' with textured milk, usually served in a glass. The amount of milk is slightly less than a Flat White but the milk is a little more textured, like a Latte. It's about half espresso and half milk.

People often think it is the same as a Flat White, and it's true there's very little difference – both are strong coffees with heated textured milk. The only real differences are that a Cortado is often made with a single shot of espresso, the milk texture is not the same and slightly less milk is used if we are going to split hairs. In cafés, it may also be served in a glass or cup not filled to the top to denote the difference. The milk takes the edge off the espresso, and the texture also gives a little feeling of luxury at the same time. Great for those in a hurry or anyone who is after a very strong but luxurious, creamy hit.

INGREDIENTS

- 1 double or 1 single shot of espresso
- 80–100ml (2¾–3½fl oz) heated textured milk

METHOD

Extract the espresso into a 175ml (6fl oz) cup or glass and fill three-quarters of the way to the top with heated textured milk (see pages 26–9).

Piccolo

I call this a 'baby Latte'. Made with a single espresso with heated textured milk (like that of a Flat White), it's smaller – only filling half a 225ml (8fl oz) glass or to the top of a 125ml (4fl oz) glass. It mimics the ratio of espresso to milk in a Latte and it's so cute! It's a smooth coffee that tastes like a Latte but has less volume and a silky texture.

It is said to have originated in Sydney and Melbourne, by roasters and baristas wanting to taste quickly how a coffee is with milk, instead of making a full Flat White or Latte. It has slightly less milk than a Cortado and usually a single shot of coffee – a balanced ratio of coffee to milk for that perfect caffeine pick-me-up. It should have a nice creamy head of milk foam at the top and is consumed in a couple of delicious mouthfuls.

INGREDIENTS

- 1 single shot of espresso
- 50–90ml (2–3fl oz) heated textured milk

METHOD

Extract the espresso into a 125ml (4fl oz) glass and fill to the top with heated textured milk (see pages 26–9).

Americano

INGREDIENTS

- 1 double shot of espresso
- 200–225ml (7–8fl oz) hot water

METHOD

Extract the espresso into your cup and add the desired amount of hot water.

The widely accepted tale of the Americano's inception dates back to Italy during World War II. It was a way to mellow the intensity of Italian espresso for the American soldiers. Unlike filter coffee, the Americano is espresso-based. A clever twist is adding a splash of cold milk, not only tempering the temperature but also offering a delightful variation. An Americano is ideal for those seeking a sizable, warm espresso-based coffee without an overpowering strength.

Long Black

INGREDIENTS

- 50–100ml (2–3½fl oz) hot water
- 1 double shot of espresso

METHOD

Pour a small amount of hot water in your cup. Extract the espresso into the cup so it floats on top of the water. Serve with a small jug of hot water (optional).

Some mistakenly dub it an Americano, but the Long Black was championed by Kiwis and packs a more robust punch than the Americano. A modest 100ml (3½fl oz) or less of hot water is added to the cup *before* the extraction of the double espresso, which delicately rests on top, allowing the attractive fresh crema to settle on top and be enjoyed. Tailored for aficionados of potent black coffee, this brew allows a leisurely sip without the brevity of an espresso shot – perfect for those on the go who still want to savour their coffee just a touch longer.

During my café-opening days, this was my morning ritual: first 'dial in' the coffee (fine-tune how much coffee to use in a perfect espresso), then relish a Long Black. In New Zealand, and now in other places around the world that have adopted it, a Long Black is often served short, with a small jug of extra hot water on the side as standard, so you can add more water to the coffee yourself at the beginning or as you go. It pairs delightfully with a sweet treat during a productive afternoon break and is considered a coffee for 'serious coffee drinkers'.

Mocha

Let me take you back to the ultimate original gateway coffee – the Mocha. It's my personal coffee origin story, set back in my teenage days, tagging along with my more 'adult' siblings on their nightly café escapades. These were our post-dinner hangouts, where they'd indulge in coffee and what felt like grown-up snacks – spicy potato wedges with soured cream or a slice of Black Forest gâteau. It felt so sophisticated, it was hard not to be enchanted. And even though I was probably pushing the coffee 'age limit', they allowed me to ditch my usual hot chocolate for a drink they called the Mochaccino, because the waiter said it had chocolate in it. It was my first taste of the coffee world's sophistication and, to this day, the Mocha remains my original coffee love.

Combining coffee and chocolate, usually hot with Latte-style milk, is a great entry into the world of coffee – I am evidence of that! I love how a Mocha can be dressed up with cream, marshmallows or pretzel sticks too. Chocolate and coffee are such a classic combination and seem to balance each other out almost perfectly.

When I first started working in a speciality café many years ago in New Zealand – the Strictly Coffee Company, a known 'purist' coffee shop – my bosses called the Mochaccino a 'Borgia' on the menu. They told me that the word meant 'to poison' in Italian... whether true or not, it was a word of warning that we are poisoning a coffee with chocolate! Today I still love and laugh with fondness at their purist attitude. I'm sure I'd often disappoint them by taking things too far, making it cold with ice or at times even adding the decadence of ice cream to my coffee!

Hot chocolate powder, especially Cadbury's, is quite sweet, so you could opt for a good-quality cocoa powder if you prefer. Chopped chocolate is more luxe.

INGREDIENTS

- 2 teaspoons hot chocolate powder or 1–2 tablespoons grated chocolate, plus extra for sprinkling
- 1 single shot of espresso
- 150–200ml (5–7fl oz) heated textured milk

METHOD

Mix the chocolate powder with the espresso in a 225–350ml (8–12fl oz) cup to form a smooth paste. Vigorously add your heated textured milk (see pages 26–9) to combine, then dust with chocolate powder. You can give it a stir before drinking.

Vienna

INGREDIENTS

- 1 single or 1 double shot of espresso, depending on your preference
- Extra hot water (optional)
- Cream, whipped to soft peaks
- White sugar or cocoa powder, for dusting

METHOD

Extract the espresso into a glass, adding hot water at this stage if you want it. Add a generous dollop of whipped cream on top. Sprinkle a nice layer of white sugar or cocoa powder on top of the cream, depending on your mood.

Eat with a spoon or drink as normal, trying to capture a touch of all the elements in each mouthful.

This, along with the 'gateway Mocha', is a memory from my very first café job. If my boss saw we needed a pick-me-up or wanted to change the mood, she'd ask us to extract a single shot of espresso into a small 125ml (4fl oz) glass. We always had a bowl of perfectly whipped cream on the go that her mum Jude (the café cook) would prepare to go with whatever cake was on offer that afternoon. A large dollop of cream would be plonked on top of the espresso, and then a sprinkling of white sugar on top, to be eaten with a spoon. As I reminisce, my mouth is watering. It's hard to describe the satisfying crunch of the crystallized sugar offsetting the bitterness of the coffee, and combining with the smoothness of the cream perfectly balancing the whole experience. It felt like an angel on a cloud, embracing the warm sun.

Slightly more pragmatically, its origins are said to come from travelling coachmen who used the cream to keep the coffee warm and minimize spillage. A traditional Viennese coffee has hot water added to the espresso, with milk and cream on top, dusted with cocoa powder or sugar.

**Coffees that take the bother
out of hot days.**

Hot
Days

2

Cold Brew

Once upon a time, baristas would have hesitated, even winced, at the idea of cold coffee.
But it is now universally embraced, and rightly so. Iced coffee and cold brew are very popular in sunnier climates, but have also found a place in many homes because of their versatility and refreshing taste, whatever the weather. Making cold brew at home is very simple and just requires a little prep the day or night before.

Cold brew uses cold or room-temperature water to brew the coffee, which gives a different quality to the flavour as the compounds are less soluble at a lower temperature, compared to hot-water brewing, which oxidizes and degrades much more, and faster. This means it's a slower process than making iced coffee – you have to increase extracting or brewing time to maximize the solubility (strength) of the coffee grounds. But a 'proper' cold brew is worth the wait.

Cold-brew ratios are generally stronger than hot-water brewing to account for reduced solubility and the addition of ice, which dilutes the drink. It can be anything between 1:7 and 1:12 coffee to water. The cold-brew method also lowers the acidity and bitterness of the coffee - it should have a strong flavour and depth.

INGREDIENTS

- 60g (2¼oz) medium- or coarse-ground coffee
- 500ml (18fl oz) filtered water
- Ice cubes (optional)
- Milk (optional)
- Sugar (optional)

METHOD

Put the freshly ground coffee in a cafetière or mason jar. Add the ice, then the water (cold or at room temperature). Cover and refrigerate for 12-24 hours.

Filter the coffee. If using a cafetière, press the filter down slowly. Or pass the coffee through a paper filter for extra clarity. Put a handful of ice in a glass and pour over your cold brew. Add milk and sugar to taste, or water to dilute.

Cold-brew Coffee Concentrate

This uses a 1:5 coffee to water ratio. You can dilute it as necessary, or simply sip it over ice.

INGREDIENTS

- 100g (3½oz) medium-ground coffee
- 500ml (18fl oz) filtered water
- Ice cubes (optional)

METHOD

Combine the ground coffee with the water, then rest in the refrigerator for 12-24 hours. Filter through a muslin cloth or paper coffee filter for a very concentrated cold brew. Dilute as necessary or serve over ice.

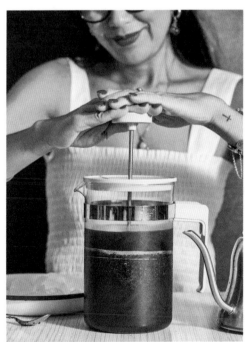

Iced Coffee

Despite their similarities, there are differences between iced coffee and cold brew. Iced coffee is basically espresso cooled down, served over ice. An Iced Americano, for example, would be espresso over ice with cold water added. An Iced Latte would be espresso over ice with cold milk added.

Iced Latte

This is a refreshing alternative to a traditional hot Latte. If you want to sweeten it, instead of the simple syrup you could sweeten the coffee with sugar while it's hot.

INGREDIENTS

• Ice cubes
• 1 double shot of espresso
• Milk
• 2–4 teaspoons Simple Syrup (see page 184 – optional)

METHOD

Place a generous amount of ice in a glass. Pour the hot espresso over the ice – espresso from a capsule espresso machine works well here, too. Top with your choice of milk and add a dash (or more) of simple syrup to sweeten if you like.

Cheat's Cold Brew

This is a quick way to make something akin to cold brew. Brew a strong pourover or filter coffee (see pages 20–3), using 25–30g (1oz) of coffee to 300ml (10fl oz) of water. This is stronger than usual because it will dilute slightly with the ice. Leave to cool at room temperature or in the refrigerator.

INGREDIENTS

• Ice cubes
• 300ml (10fl oz) strong filter coffee, cooled
• Milk (optional)
• Simple Syrup (see page 184 – optional)

METHOD

Place a generous amount of ice in a glass and add the strong filter coffee. Drink it black or add a splash of milk and sugar syrup to taste.

Iced Mocha

Similar to a Mocha, but iced! If you're feeling indulgent, add some ice cream. It's great on a low day when you need a pick-me-up, and it's so simple to make at home using just chocolate or cocoa powder and espresso.

The chocolate sauce can be made with 3–4 teaspoons of hot chocolate powder dissolved into 30ml (1fl oz) of boiling water. Alternatively, you can use store-bought chocolate sauce or chocolate or hazelnut spread loosened with boiling water.

INGREDIENTS

- 30ml (1fl oz) chocolate sauce
- Ice cubes
- 1 double shot of espresso
- 1 generous scoop of chocolate, vanilla or espresso ice cream (optional)
- 150–200ml (5–7fl oz) milk of your choice
- Hot chocolate powder or orange zest, to garnish

METHOD

Smear the chocolate sauce around the insides of the glass. Add some ice – do not fill the glass, just add enough to cover the bottom and cool the drink.

Pour the espresso over the ice to flash cool, then add the ice cream (optional but highly recommended). Slowly add the milk to the top of the glass and stir with a spoon. Dust with chocolate or garnish with orange zest and enjoy.

Irish Cream Iced Coffee

Good Irish cream liqueur complements coffee and milk exceptionally well, making it a standout choice for any gathering, be it a house party or a dinner party – or even a cheeky quiet moment on your own once the kids are in bed! The best-known and most widely available Irish cream is Baileys and it comes in many variations (including a plant-based version) that are fun to experiment with. The coffee works its magic by balancing out the sweetness of the liqueur, offering a delightful experience whether served hot or cold.

If you prefer an extra chill, try shaking the concoction in a cocktail shaker, then strain it into your favourite cocktail glass, or follow the simple build method I've employed here. Crafting an Irish Cream Iced Coffee is effortlessly easy and presents beautifully.

INGREDIENTS

- Ice cubes
- 150ml (5fl oz) cold brew or cooled strong filter coffee (see page 52 or 55)
- 50ml (2fl oz) Irish cream liqueur, such as Baileys
- 50ml (2fl oz) milk or cream (optional)

METHOD

Fill a glass with ice. Pour the cold coffee into the glass, add the liqueur and stir. Add milk or maybe some cheeky cream if you like, and enjoy.

Coffee Granita

I first tried granita in Melbourne when I moved there after graduating from university. Australia's coffee evolution has been heavily shaped by the influence of Italian immigrants, particularly in Melbourne. From the use of espresso machines to coffee serves, a strong Italian culture lives on. They even have a Little Italy there and the granita is one of those serves you can rely on to cool you down on an insanely hot Melbourne summer's day. Granita, which originated in Sicily, is traditionally made from water, sugar and fruit. Coffee granita can be made easily at home, by substituting coffee for fruit.

You need 500ml (18fl oz) of strong coffee for this recipe. You want the coffee to be very strong because when it freezes, it loses some of its intensity. Use 60g (2¼oz) of coffee with the cold-brew method or make multiple brews in a moka pot. Alternatively, put the ground coffee in a saucepan with the water and bring almost to a boil, then strain through a paper coffee filter or muslin cloth and cool.

INGREDIENTS

- **500ml (18fl oz) strong brewed coffee**
- **2 teaspoons honey or agave syrup**
- **Zest of 1 lemon or lime**
- **Condensed milk** (optional)
- **Dark spiced rum** (optional)

METHOD

Make the coffee, dissolve the honey or syrup in it, add a generous sprinkling of finely grated lemon or lime zest and leave to cool to room temperature. Pour into a shallow freezer-proof tray or container and cover.

Place in the freezer and check every 30-60 minutes; once ice crystals start to form, scrape it with a fork to break up the crystals and mix well. Repeat every 30-60 minutes until frozen; this should take about 4 hours. This is the traditional way to make granita and produces the best result.

Alternatively, just freeze the mixture until solid and 30 minutes before you're ready to serve, take it out of the freezer to soften slightly, then give it a rough chop in a blender or food processor until it forms icy flakes. Or you can freeze it in a strong sealable bag and give it a light smash on the ground to break up the frozen coffee, though the texture isn't *as* good.

Whichever method you use, once it's loosened you can keep it in the freezer until needed. It will now break up more easily on serving.

Serve the granita in glasses. To add a little decadence, drizzle some condensed milk around the glass for extra pizazz and to offset any bitterness. To adult it up, add a dash of dark spiced rum.

Caramel Frappé

'Frappé' is a French term used to describe a drink that is chilled with ice and shaken or blended. There are different accounts as to who invented the Frappé, but it seems it was created in 1957 by a Nescafé rep at a trade show. In the mid 1990s, the Starbucks coffee chain trademarked the term 'Frappuccino', so now 'Frappé' is used everywhere else. The growth of Starbucks around the world enabled consumers wide accessibility to such drinks and the Frappé quickly became very popular. Who doesn't love a fun, icy, sugary, creamy coffee?

There are many iterations of a Frappuccino or Frappé, allowing creativity with toppings and sauces, so feel free to get your creative hat on and dream up your own wonderful variations of my recipe below. Use store-bought caramel sauce or make your own (see page 187), or substitute the caramel for chocolate or hazelnut sauce or a tablespoon of Nutella. You can also try any of these toppings: Oreos or other cookies, sprinkles, marshmallows, grated chocolate, berries or other fruit, Smarties or M&Ms, wafer rolls (piroulines), or toffee chunks.

INGREDIENTS

- 2 double shots of espresso
- 2 large handfuls of ice cubes
- 150ml (5fl oz) milk
- 2 tablespoons caramel sauce, plus extra to decorate
- Cream, whipped to soft peaks
- Hot chocolate powder or ground cinnamon, to dust

METHOD

Place the coffee, ice and milk in a blender and blend well. Line the insides of your glass with the caramel sauce and pour in the coffee. Top with whipped cream, squiggle caramel sauce on top and dust with chocolate or cinnamon.

Affogato

This is essentially one scoop of ice cream with a double shot of espresso on top. The name translates as 'drowned', depicting the ice cream being submerged in espresso. It's a delightful dessert of indulgence, especially in the warmth of summer. The blend of coffee and sweet, creamy ice cream creates a harmonious texture, which manages to feel both luxurious and straightforward at the same time. Vanilla ice cream is always a good option – the creamier the better – or use coffee ice cream (see page 177). A great no-fuss dessert if you're ever stuck last minute. You can top with chopped nuts or grated chocolate, or serve with biscuits or wafers.

INGREDIENTS

- 1 double shot of espresso
- 1 scoop of ice cream of your choice
- Grated chocolate, nuts, wafers or mini ice cream cones (optional)

METHOD

Prepare your espresso in a small cup or jug. In a larger cup, glass or small bowl, place the scoop of ice cream. Pour the espresso over your ice cream and enjoy with a spoon!

Serve your Affogato with grated chocolate, nuts, wafers or mini ice cream cones for extra indulgence.

Coffee Radler

There was a time when I had friends in Berlin so I visited them frequently. The city boasts numerous excellent speciality cafés and the quality of locally roasted coffee is impressive. You might recognize some well-known favourites like The Barn, Five Elephant and Bonanza Coffee. While I haven't experienced Oktoberfest in Munich myself yet, I'm well aware that beer is a popular everyday drink (after coffee, of course). In Germany, a beloved summer beverage is the Radler beer and many craft beer brands worldwide have created their own versions. It's a refreshing drink similar to a shandy, where lemonade and lemon are added to beer. The unique aspect of a Radler is its 50 per cent beer and 50 per cent citrus-flavoured soda requirement (using lemon, orange, lime or grapefruit).

Here's my take on a Radler, incorporating coffee! I know beer and coffee might seem a bit strange, but it's a rather different, thirst-quenching and fun option for low-alcohol friends. Try it with your favourite fruit soda. Best enjoyed on a sunny day outdoors.

INGREDIENTS

- 50–75ml (2–2½fl oz) cold-brew coffee or 1 double shot of espresso, cooled
- 150ml (5fl oz) cold lager
- Ice (optional)
- Fruit-flavoured soda, such as orange, lemon, raspberry or grapefruit, to top up
- Citrus wedge, to garnish

METHOD

Place the coffee and lager in a 300ml (10fl oz) glass. Add the ice (if using) and top up with your favourite fruit-flavoured soda. Add a citrus wedge – I like to use grapefruit – then serve.

**Coffee cocktails and evening
favourites.**

Nights

3

Coffee cocktails

The world of cocktails has seen an incredible surge in creativity and variety. Coffee cocktails, especially the Espresso Martini, have taken centre stage in this evolution. This versatile drink has become a go-to before dinner, during dinner and after dinner, inspiring various interpretations that smoothly transition coffee from day to night. The Espresso Martini carries an exciting and slightly naughty vibe, suggesting a night of lively partying and dancing. The coffee flavour is heightened, and the vodka adds a distinct kick without compromising the purist essence of the drink.

Whether you're planning a cosy evening at home or spontaneously whipping up a batch of cocktails for a dinner party, here are some tips.

It's important to note that measurements of alcohol differ slightly worldwide. I use a jigger, which is a bar tool with pre-measured 'single' and 'double' shots. In the southern hemisphere, for example, single shots can be 15ml (½fl oz) and double shots 30ml (1fl oz). I found that when I moved to London the drinks were SO much stronger. But now, after many years, it's quite standard. For the purpose of this book and my recipes, 25–30ml (1fl oz) is fine for a standard shot of alcohol. A double shot (depending on what measuring tool you're using) will be double the amount of the single shot, so 50–60ml (2–2¼fl oz). If it's a little less or a little more, it shouldn't make too much difference as long as the ratios are relatively similar.

When I refer to a double shot of espresso, it should be 30–50ml (1–2fl oz), usually using 15–20g (½–¾oz) of coffee. Opt for high-quality espresso whenever possible. If you're fortunate to own an automatic bean-to-cup espresso machine, crafting a late-night Espresso Martini becomes effortlessly tempting. I swear by my Melitta bean-to-cup machines; they're user- and budget-friendly, and churn out coffee from fresh beans, which is my preference when making an espresso or multiple martinis. When a swift espresso is needed for a recipe, it's just a matter of a button press after turning it on. But there are plenty of other options. For a heartier brew, I turn to a more commercial-grade home machine, like the La Marzocco Mini or Micra for example. While quality is very important to me, I acknowledge I'm privileged that my career affords me top-notch equipment, but I also believe that any home espresso experience is a luxury, irrespective of the machine!

Another innovative sector making waves is the capsule or pod market, offering unparalleled convenience, especially in cocktails. Depending on the pods you choose, the strength and flavour may vary, but they are quick and perfectly suited for your home cocktails. It's crucial to bear in mind that coffee pods or capsules generally contain around 5–7g (about ⅛oz) of coffee, limiting both taste and strength to some extent. Having experimented with various brands, I've found that the speciality market produces better-tasting capsules of higher quality without an overwhelming dark, burnt flavour. Despite this, the robust flavours you find in some pod brands can work well in cocktails, where alcohol helps mask some overpowering notes. Additionally, pod coffee does maintain its freshness for much longer than coffee beans due to the nitrogen flushing that removes oxygen from the packaging and the sealed containers preventing oxygen degradation. Make sure you opt for compostable or eco-friendly pods where possible.

For those concerned about consuming caffeine late at night, excellent decaffeinated coffee options are available. Keeping some decaf coffee beans or decaf pods to hand can be a smart choice for crafting delightful late-night cocktails (or mocktails).

Many of the following cocktail recipes require coffee liqueur for their flavour – there's a recipe on page 182 to make your own, or try Kahlúa, Tia Maria or Mr Black.

Espresso Martini ①

INGREDIENTS

- Ice cubes
- 1 double shot of espresso
- 50ml (2fl oz) vodka
- 30ml (1fl oz) coffee liqueur
- 15ml (½fl oz) Simple Syrup (see page 184)
- 3 coffee beans, to garnish

METHOD

Fill a cocktail shaker with ice, add the coffee, then add the vodka, coffee liqueur and syrup. Shake very vigorously to make sure you get a thick foam on top. Strain into a glass and garnish with the quintessential 3 coffee beans on the thick foam.

People go crazy for Espresso Martinis. Some people who don't even like coffee LOVE these cocktails. Why wouldn't they? They're sweet but balanced and have a kick that makes them fun! It's hard *not* to get excited about an Espresso Martini. If you are hosting or going to a dinner party, you can extract some espresso earlier in the day and store it in the refrigerator ready for cocktail hour. Generally, you'll need to extract 30ml (1fl oz) of espresso per cocktail. If it is hot, add it to the shaker first to allow it to cool with the ice. This recipe makes one cocktail.

Some fun variations on the classic...

- **Chilli Espresso Martini ②**: add 1 small, or ½ a large, chopped red chilli to the shaker with the other ingredients and strain out with the ice. Garnish with slices of fresh red chilli, rim the glass with chilli powder or flakes, or add a whole chilli to the edge of the glass for extra flair.

- **Vanilla & Apple Brandy Espresso Martini ③**: substitute the vodka with apple or cider brandy and add a drop of vanilla extract. Garnish with apple slices and a dusting of ground cinnamon.

- **Rum & Lime Espresso Martini ④**: add ½ teaspoon of ground cardamom and 15ml (½fl oz) lime juice. Substitute the vodka with spiced rum, such as Captain Morgan. Garnish with a dusting of ground cardamom or cardamom seeds.

Caramel Macchiato Martini

You can use homemade caramel sauce (like the Salted Espresso Caramel on page 187), but store-bought is fine as long as it is thick but runny enough to run down the sides of the glass.

INGREDIENTS

- 1 tablespoon caramel sauce, plus extra to garnish
- Ice cubes
- 1 double shot of espresso
- 50ml (2fl oz) vodka
- 25–30ml (1fl oz) coffee liqueur
- Cream, whipped to soft peaks
- 1 coffee bean, to garnish

METHOD

Line the insides of the glass with caramel sauce. Fill a cocktail shaker with ice, add the espresso, vodka and coffee liqueur, and shake well. Strain into your prepared glass. Gently float a dainty spoonful of whipped cream on top, squiggle caramel sauce over the cream and add a coffee bean to garnish.

Mocha Martini

Coffee and chocolate may go down as one of the greatest relationships of all time. Hot, cold, day, night, anything's possible with this pair.

The two flavours balance each other out perfectly in this drink, and it's a great alternative to a straight up espresso martini.

INGREDIENTS

- Ice cubes
- 1 double shot of espresso
- 50ml (2fl oz) vodka
- 25–30ml (1fl oz) coffee liqueur
- 1 tablespoon chocolate sauce or chocolate liqueur
- Grated chocolate and chocolate-covered coffee beans, to garnish

METHOD

Fill a cocktail shaker with ice, add the espresso, vodka, coffee liqueur and chocolate sauce or liqueur, and shake well. Double strain into a glass and garnish with grated chocolate and chocolate-covered coffee beans.

④ Rum & Lime Espresso Martini

① Espresso Martini

② Chilli Espresso Martini

③ Vanilla & Apple Brandy Espresso Martini

Flat White Martini

While the Espresso Martini is enjoyed all year round, this Flat White Martini is perhaps a little more seasonal with its use of Irish cream liqueur. This drink is great in place of, or with, a dessert if you have company and want to make your guests feel a little special and excited. Pour into a Martini glass, a Nick and Nora glass or a coupe. Dust some cocoa powder on top and it will look just like a delicious dessert.

To go that one step further, make some Tiramisu Latte mascarpone cream (see page 107) and slap some on the rim of the glass, garnishing with a Biscoff or lady finger biscuit.

METHOD

Fill a cocktail shaker with ice, add the coffee, vodka, coffee liqueur and Irish cream liqueur. Shake very vigorously to make sure you get a thick foam on top, then strain into a glass. Add coffee beans, to garnsh.

INGREDIENTS

- Ice cubes
- 1 double shot of espresso
- 30ml (1fl oz) vodka
- 30ml (1fl oz) coffee liqueur
- 50ml (2fl oz) Irish cream liqueur, such as Baileys
- Coffee beans, to garnish

Espresso Tonic

This is great on a warm evening and very refreshing. It's non-alcoholic and the bubbles are so thirst quenching, but the espresso element is obviously the best flavour! Sometimes if it's not on the menu at a café, I'll order an espresso and a bottle of sparkling water or tonic with a glass of ice and lemon and build one there and then. It's the perfect summer drink to make at home.

If you want to make it Christmassy or more suited to a special occasion, it's a great alternative to a Mimosa. Rim a Champagne flute with agave syrup and ground cinnamon, replace the tonic water with chilled Champagne or prosecco and garnish with a star anise, a sprig of rosemary or a cherry.

INGREDIENTS

- Ice cubes
- 1 double shot of espresso
- 125–175ml (4–6fl oz) tonic water
- Squeeze of lime or orange peel twist, to garnish

METHOD

Fill a 200ml (7fl oz) glass with ice, then add the espresso. Alternatively, you can use 30–45ml (1–1½fl oz) strong AeroPress coffee or concentrated cold brew. Top up with tonic and add a small squeeze of lime or an orange peel twist to garnish. Squeezing the orange oils on top of the glass gives it a lovely aroma.

Coffee G&T

METHOD

For a Coffee G&T, follow the recipe above, but add 30ml (1fl oz) of gin with the espresso before topping up the glass with tonic. You could also substitute the tonic with soda water and a squeeze of lemon.

Coffee Negroni

Negronis – you either love them or hate them. I love them, especially the bold flavours and the bitter-sweet balance. But when you add coffee, it is next level! Coffee mellows out the sweetness of the drink and, at the same time, enhances the flavours. Make sure to use a filter coffee or cold brew as they're more delicate – espresso would be too overpowering.

A Negroni is made with equal parts of gin, vermouth and Campari built over a solid block of ice and stirred so that it is slightly diluted. Ideally, the ice doesn't melt too fast! There are two ways to make a Coffee Negroni – the first is by simply adding cold coffee to your cocktail (see below), the other is by infusing the vermouth with ground coffee and making a Negroni in the usual way (see page 183).

METHOD

Place the ice in a glass and add the other ingredients one by one to build the cocktail. Stir and enjoy. If you'd prefer it less strong, you could add tonic water to dilute it a little. Garnish with an orange peel twist, if you like.

INGREDIENTS

- 1 large piece of ice
- 50ml (2fl oz) gin
- 50ml (2fl oz) sweet vermouth
- 50ml (2fl oz) Campari
- 20ml (¾fl oz) cold brew or strong filter coffee
- Tonic water, to dilute (optional)
- Orange peel twist, to garnish (optional)

Coffee Old Fashioned

INGREDIENTS

- Ice cubes
- 50ml (2fl oz) bourbon or rye whiskey
- 50ml (2fl oz) cold filter coffee
- 1 teaspoon Demerara Syrup (see page 184 – or more to taste)
- 2–3 dashes of Angostura bitters (or orange bitters)
- Orange peel twist, to garnish

METHOD

Place some ice in a glass and add the whiskey and coffee. Stir in the sugar syrup, then add the bitters. Garnish with a simple orange peel twist, spritzing the oil over the drink first for extra flavour.

The Old Fashioned is possibly one of the most iconic cocktails globally. Bourbon and whisky, once an acquired taste, have grown on me as I have delved into the intricacies of their crafting and flavours. My whisky journey took a formal turn when I worked with The Macallan, a top-tier distillery nestled in the north-east of Scotland. It all started with their release of coffee whisky – not coffee-infused, but inspired by the parallels between the worlds of coffee and whisky. From bean to cup or grain to glass, both products follow a similar journey that unlocks incredibly interesting and complex flavours.

I always get a little confused as to its spelling, so I've laid it out here in case you do too. 'Whiskey' (spelled with an 'e') is used in the USA and Ireland, while 'whisky' (without an 'e') is usually used in Scotland and Canada. The name depends on the cereal grain, distilling process and how and where it is produced. Bourbon and rye whiskey must have a certain amount of corn mash (bourbon), rye mash or rye malt mash and both must be made in the United States. It sounds complicated, but luckily it's much easier to drink (or sip) with coffee I find!

Caramel White Choc Hit

Who doesn't like a little decadence in their Latte? This is an easy treat to make at home after dinner when you have caramel sauce in the cupboard, or a small bit of leftover chocolate. To be honest, you can use any flavour chocolate you like and the quantities are not crucial. Enjoy with a dunked Flat White Cookie (see page 164) or Coffee Shortbread (see page 168).

INGREDIENTS

- White chocolate, finely chopped or grated
- Caramel sauce
- 1 double shot of espresso
- Heated textured milk

METHOD

Place the white chocolate and caramel sauce in a cup or glass, then add the freshly brewed espresso. Using a teaspoon, mix the ingredients together until they are a little melted. Pour in your hot frothy milk and top with some squiggles of caramel sauce and grated chocolate on top.

Double Black Russian

INGREDIENTS

- Ice cubes
- 50–60ml (2–2¼fl oz) vodka
- 25–30ml (1fl oz) coffee liqueur
- 25–30ml (1fl oz) espresso or cold brew
- Dash of orange bitters (optional)
- Cola (optional)

METHOD

Place some ice in a glass and add the vodka, coffee liqueur and coffee, and stir. Add a dash of bitters and top with cola if you like – it gives it a likeness to a glass of stout.

This cocktail is based on the classic Black Russian, which is very simple – 2 parts vodka to 1 part coffee liqueur, such as Kahlúa, Tia Maria or Mr Black. However, I always prefer to add a shot of coffee, whether it's an espresso or some cold brew. Cold brew is less acidic and lighter, which I prefer in this cocktail. It offsets the sweetness of the liqueur and takes the edge off the vodka.

Classic White Russian

INGREDIENTS

- Ice cubes
- 50ml (2fl oz) vodka
- 25–30ml (1fl oz) coffee liqueur
- 30ml (1fl oz) espresso or 30–50ml (1–2fl oz) cold brew (optional)
- 30ml (1fl oz) cream

METHOD

Place some ice in a glass and add the vodka, coffee liqueur and coffee (if using), and stir. Slowly stir in the cream.

A White Russian is made with vodka, coffee liqueur and cream, gently stirred through. It's the cream that creates a dramatic effect and really rounds off the sharpness of the vodka and balances the sweetness of the coffee liqueur. It's an enjoyable and decadent drink. For a seasonal take on this drink, see page 103.

Coffee Mint Julep

This easy take on the traditional Mint Julep is wonderful. The coffee really brings out depth and smooths out the flavour of the mint and bourbon. It's lovely and one of my favourites to sip. The bitters certainly give it a zing!

INGREDIENTS

- **6–8 mint leaves,** plus extra to garnish
- **15ml (½fl oz) Simple Syrup** (see page 184) **or honey**
- **Ice cubes**
- **30ml (1fl oz) espresso, cold brew or strong filter coffee**
- **50ml (2fl oz) bourbon**
- **Angostura bitters**
- **Lemon or orange zest and edible flowers,** to garnish (optional)

METHOD

Place the mint in a cocktail shaker with the sugar syrup. Muddle together. Add ice, then the coffee. Add the bourbon and shake vigorously. Either serve over crushed ice, or simply strain into a Nick and Nora glass. Garnish with mint leaves, a splash of bitters and citrus zest. I like to add edible flowers too, for some extra flair.

Rum & Coke Espresso

Rum and Coke is said to have originated in Cuba during the Spanish-American war, when soldiers stationed there mixed Coca-Cola with Bacardi rum and a squeeze of lime. As a student, I often saw people drinking it – it seemed like a really easy option to order and drink, because of the sweetness of the cola. It's even easier to make at home, but with a little extra pizazz – adding espresso tastes really good! Coca-Cola is obviously the classic, but now there are many other colas with really interesting spicy herbal flavours to them that you could try for that artisanal touch. The espresso creates more balance for the sweetness and causes the drink to fizz somewhat, which is visually exciting. The head on it resembles that on a glass of Guinness or stout.

INGREDIENTS

- **Ice cubes**
- **50ml (2fl oz) dark spiced rum or white Bacardi rum**
- **1 double shot of espresso**
- **100ml (3½fl oz) cola**
- **Lime wedge or orange peel**

METHOD

Place a handful of ice in a glass. Add the rum and espresso, then top slowly with cola. Garnish with a lime wedge or orange peel.

Espresso Bellini

This drink is a special and fancy take on a Champagne breakfast, and can be enjoyed in the evening too. Instead of the traditional peach, it involves adding coffee ice cubes to prosecco or Champagne, because it's no proper breakfast without coffee! I have often served this on Christmas morning, but it would be a great tradition on Mother's Day, Father's Day, birthdays or any kind of celebration. It's a little different but so comfortingly familiar and looks special.

INGREDIENTS

- 300ml (10fl oz) cold brew or strong filter coffee
- Agave syrup or honey
- Ground cinnamon (optional)
- Prosecco or Champagne

METHOD

Freeze the coffee in an ice cube tray to make small cubes. Dip the rims of the Champagne flutes in agave syrup or honey and roll in a little cinnamon (optional). Place 3-4 coffee ice cubes in each glass and slowly pour in the prosecco or Champagne. If you prefer, add the coffee cubes last for more fizz!

Coffee Margarita Sunset

The enchanting allure of a Margarita – a true elixir of joy. While tequila may not be my forte, there's an undeniable magic when it joins forces with tacos. Fond memories linger of an unforgettable taco and margarita affair in Los Angeles, curated by Bill Esparza. It showcased a delicious introduction for me into the vibrant world of Mexican flavours, offering the best tacos in the city – a quintessential part of the LA experience. Naturally, authentic Margaritas flowed.

Though I love the tangy embrace of a Margarita, I can't take too many. Introducing coffee into this established cocktail adds a somewhat nuanced element on the palate. Picture a ripple of cold brew or cold filter delicately floating on top, offering not only a visual feast but a sophisticated taste to elevate the experience. I surprised even myself with how much I love this one.

INGREDIENTS

- Salt
- Ice cubes
- 15ml (½fl oz) agave syrup
- 30ml (1fl oz) lime juice
- 30ml (1fl oz) Cointreau or triple sec
- 50ml (2fl oz) tequila blanco or reposado
- 30ml (1fl oz) strong cold brew, filter coffee or espresso, cooled

METHOD

Salt the rim of a chilled glass and add some ice. Fill a cocktail shaker with ice, add the syrup, lime juice, Cointreau and tequila, and shake. Double strain into the glass and float the coffee on top – go for a cold brew if you are after a delicate, refined look.

S'mores Please!

Winter nights conjure thoughts of camping or, in my case, sitting by a cozy fire (much more appealing than setting up a tent) or your favourite candles. S'mores are the epitome of fancy camping but who said you can't just have them in the comfort of your own home? Who can resist a perfectly toasted marshmallow and what could be more luxurious than having one with a beautiful cup of coffee? The perfect luxe pairing.

All you need are a few simple tools. Grab a kitchen blow torch or just use the gas flame on your stove top. But remember, play it safe. Don't let those marshmallows catch fire and always be cautious around open flames. Use store-bought caramel sauce or the Salted Espresso Caramel on page 187. Let the indoor camping (and caffeinated S'mores) adventures begin!

METHOD

Smear the jam roughly around the inside of a 225–350ml (8–12fl oz) mug so it shows strong flashes of red. Add your espresso and caramel sauce, then pour the milk into the mug.

For that campfire feel, place 2–3 medium marshmallows or 1 very large one on a short skewer and lightly toast. Place the skewer on top of the mug and sprinkle with crushed cookie and dried raspberry pieces or a whole fresh raspberry.

INGREDIENTS

- 1 tablespoon raspberry jam
- 1 double shot of espresso
- 30ml (1fl oz) caramel sauce
- 150–200ml (5–7fl oz) heated textured milk
- 2–3 medium marshmallows or 1 very large one
- 1 cookie, crushed
- Freeze-dried raspberry pieces or 1 fresh raspberry, to garnish

**Quintessential seasonal serves
to make at home.**

Seasonal
Favourites

4

Pumpkin Spice Latte

This is a popular choice in the autumn months. It is often made with a flavoured pumpkin spice syrup, which can be bought from the supermarket or online, but it's very easy to make your own using some pumpkin purée, spices and a simple syrup to sweeten it. Use pumpkin purée from a can, or make your own by boiling some peeled pumpkin until soft, then puréeing in a blender.

INGREDIENTS

- 30ml (1fl oz) Simple Syrup (see page 184)
- 1 double shot of espresso
- 2 teaspoons pumpkin purée
- 200ml (7fl oz) milk
- Ground cinnamon or grated nutmeg
- Roasted pumpkin slices and pumpkin seeds, to garnish (optional)
- 1 cinnamon stick (optional)

METHOD

Put the syrup and espresso in a mug.

Place the puréed pumpkin and milk in a milk jug and steam until hot and frothy. Alternatively, use a milk frother – just make sure that the purée is really smooth.

Pour your heated textured milk into the mug and dust with cinnamon or nutmeg. If you like, garnish with roasted pumpkin slices and pumpkin seeds or a cinnamon stick across your glass. For extra effect, you can singe the ends of the stick with a kitchen blow torch, gas flame or lighter, but please be careful around flames.

Gingerbread Latte

Autumn and winter coffees can be even more interesting and fun with warming spices. Just like with the Pumpkin Spice Latte on page 99, this can be made with spices from scratch – or use 1 tablespoon of shop-bought syrup or the Ginger Syrup on page 184 in place of the spices and sugar in this recipe if you prefer. This style of drink is popular during the colder months and you could make it visually fun with mini gingerbread men served alongside to dip in!

INGREDIENTS

- ½ teaspoon ground ginger, plus extra for dusting
- ¼ teaspoon ground cinnamon
- Small pinch of grated nutmeg
- 1–2 teaspoons soft brown sugar
- 2 drops of vanilla extract
- 1 double shot of espresso
- 250ml (9fl oz) heated textured milk
- Cream, whipped to soft peaks
- Crushed ginger cookies, to garnish

METHOD

Put the ginger, cinnamon, nutmeg, sugar and vanilla into a 300ml (10fl oz) mug or cup. Add the espresso and mix the ingredients into a syrupy paste. Pour the heated textured milk into your cup so that the syrup mixes with the milk. You can practice your Latte art if you like (see pages 26–9). Dollop some whipped cream on top and dust with ground ginger. Add some crushed ginger cookies on top for extra gingery goodness.

Christmas White Russian

INGREDIENTS

For the eggnog

- 3 egg yolks
- 30g (1oz) sugar
- 125ml (4fl oz) double cream
- 250ml (9fl oz) milk
- ¼ teaspoon grated nutmeg
- ¼ teaspoon ground cinnamon
- Pinch of salt
- ¼ teaspoon vanilla paste or scraped seeds from 1 vanilla pod
- ½ teaspoon fine-ground coffee

For the cocktail

- Agave syrup
- Ground cinnamon
- Ice cubes
- 50ml (2fl oz) vodka
- 30ml (1fl oz) coffee liqueur
- 15ml (½fl oz) Cointreau
- 30ml (1fl oz) strong cold brew or filter coffee
- Star anise or a few coffee beans
- Grated nutmeg, to garnish (optional)

To really showcase coffee (and maybe use up some leftover filter coffee), this Christmassy take on the White Russian has a fun twist – it has eggnog on top. You can substitute the Cointreau for brandy, bourbon or rum (which traditionally goes with eggnog) to give the drink a different kind of warm kick.

METHOD

First make the eggnog because it needs to cool and chill. Mix the egg yolks and sugar in a heatproof bowl. Place the cream, milk, nutmeg, cinnamon, salt, vanilla and coffee in a saucepan over a medium heat until hot, but don't let it boil. Pour this slowly over the yolk and sugar mixture, whisking all the time, then return to the saucepan to heat again until very hot, but again not boiling. Stir constantly as it thickens, then remove from the heat and pour into a bowl. Let it cool to room temperature, cover and place in the refrigerator until chilled. When you're ready to use it, give it a quick whip to aerate.

For the cocktail, rim a glass with agave and ground cinnamon. Place some ice in the glass and build the vodka, coffee liqueur, Cointreau and coffee over the ice and stir. Top with more ice if there is a lot of space in the top of the glass – you should leave about 1cm (½ inch) clear. Using the back of a spoon, float the eggnog on top of the drink. Place a star anise or a few coffee beans on top and sprinkle with nutmeg.

Christmas Cosmo

This cocktail is a sophisticated festive spin on a classic, offering a deliciously tangy yet refined flavour profile that's just as delightful all year round. This one uses gin as its base, but you can use vodka if you prefer. The coffee adds a grounding element to the festive mix, balancing out the brightness with a touch of depth. The cheeky touch of Champagne or prosecco gives it that extra bit of flair and it's a great way to use up any leftover fizz. And if you find cocktails a little strong, you can always halve the gin quantity and add more bubbles or cranberry juice to reduce the strength.

It's like the *Sex and the City* of cocktails – always classy, a little indulgent and absolutely irresistible.

METHOD

Fill a cocktail shaker with ice, then add the gin, Cointreau, lime juice, syrup, cranberry juice and coffee. Shake vigorously to create a stiff foam, strain into a martini glass and top with a splash of prosecco or Champagne. Garnish with fresh cranberries and a rosemary or mint sprig.

INGREDIENTS

- Ice cubes
- 50ml (2fl oz) gin
- 15ml (½fl oz) Cointreau
- 15ml (½fl oz) lime juice
- 15ml (½fl oz) Simple Syrup (see page 184)
- 30ml (1fl oz) cranberry juice
- 30ml (1fl oz) strong cold brew
- Prosecco or Champagne
- Fresh cranberries and a rosemary or mint sprig, to garnish

Tiramisu Latte

This is my very simple version of a Tiramisu Latte, which is replicable and easy to make. It's optional to add the rum or coffee liqueur, but it adds a subtle boozy warmth to the drink just as it does in a tiramisu dessert. And you get the creamy consistency on the top to dip a lady finger in.

INGREDIENTS

- 100g (3½oz) mascarpone
- 2 heaped tablespoons whipped cream
- 1–2 teaspoons icing sugar
- 1 tablespoon instant coffee
- 1 double shot of espresso
- 15ml (½fl oz) rum or coffee liqueur (optional)
- 300ml (10fl oz) heated textured milk
- 1 teaspoon cocoa powder
- 1 lady finger biscuit

METHOD

Fold together the mascarpone, whipped cream and icing sugar in a bowl. In a separate bowl, dissolve the instant coffee in 1 teaspoon of water and mix until it forms a paste, then fold this into the mascarpone mixture. Refrigerate and make sure it is cold when you use it.

Make your Latte as usual by pouring the espresso and liqueur (if using) into a cup and layering the milk on top. Dust heavily with cocoa powder. Use a spatula or knife to smear some of the mascarpone mixture on the lip of the cup on one side or pipe it around the rim, if you want, to make it look fancy. Place a lady finger neatly on top and dust with a little more cocoa powder.

Enjoy by scooping some of the mascarpone mixture onto the biscuit, then dip into the coffee and enjoy! I love this one.

**Just a few of my favourite
coffees from around the world.**

Coffee Traditions

Global coffee culture

I once ended a budding romance over a clash in coffee values!
I offered to treat my date to an espresso from a speciality café,
only for him to loudly protest the price, predict its sour taste
and grumble about the wait time. Not only was I mortified by
his complaints, but it made an impact because coffee has been
my lifelong career. This encounter reminded me how important
it is to be mindful of diverse perceptions, knowledge and priorities.

While I don't scrutinize every coffee experience, this incident
highlighted the impact of cultural and social references on how
people perceive coffee, in particular, speciality coffee. I wasn't
insisting that he adopt my coffee preferences, I was offering
something different to his norm, a 'treat' and, I guess, hoping
to impress... Needless to say, it left a sour taste in my coffee and
became the quirky tale of a romance that didn't quite brew right.
It's okay for people to appreciate different things due to cultural
and social influences, but always try to be open, kind and respectful.

In many cultures, the term 'coffee' encompasses a broad spectrum,
akin to the world of wine, although I consider good coffee to be an
affordable luxury, not as much a hefty investment as fine wine.

It's a pleasure and a privilege for me to travel around the world and
experience different cultures. Seeing how people live, socialize and,
of course, drink coffee. I've been so fortunate in creating a career
and life that has allowed me to explore this. I love observing habits,
styles, traditions and trends around food and coffee, from the staff
to the design and ambience of the cafés. Talking to people and
finding out more about how they live is of huge interest to me.

Being a part of the coffee and food industry, I've had access to
an incredible world that has allowed me a unique insight into this
world of business, coffee and how that fits into people's lives and
lifestyles. The following selection of recipes from various coffee
traditions is far from exhaustive. In this vast world of cultures and
traditions, these are just a few of my personal favourites, and this
list continues to grow. I'm excited to share them with you, inviting
you to embark on a delicious journey through the diverse realms of
coffee, and nudge you to incorporate some of these serves into your
daily routine. You can try these global coffees at home whenever you
feel like taking a trip around the world, or impressing *yourself*...

Turkish coffee

Turkish coffee, also known as *cezve* or *ibrik*, has roots in the Ottoman Empire. Its robust flavour, compared to 'regular' coffee, is a result of a unique brewing process involving a copper pot, rapid heat transfer, very finely ground coffee and continuous extraction. Back when coffee quality wasn't top-notch, sugar or spices like cinnamon were added to mask bitterness. And don't forget about Turkish sand coffee – where the *ibrik* (copper coffee pot) is nestled in heated sand, and the deeper it goes, the hotter the temperature, creating a distinct and fascinating brewing experience.

Being concentrated, Turkish coffee aligns more with the espresso family. This brewing method creates distinct body, lush mouthfeel from the rich crema, aromatic essence and unique flavours. The *ibrik*, often with a narrow top to let the crema bloom, has a wide base to allow coffee grounds to settle gracefully. The coffee is enjoyed in uniquely designed cups.

After savouring the slowly sipped brew, a delightful tradition unfolds. You turn the cup upside down, chat for a while and then, with a touch of ceremony, the elders honour the ancient art of coffee reading, by interpreting the image created from the coffee sediment in your cup, a bit like a horoscope!

One Christmas, I had some Turkish friends demonstrate this, placing a ring on top of my cup for a touch of romantic luck. They turned my cup back over, revealing I had 'a lot of luck', determined by the length of time it took the coffee sludge to slide out. Having my coffee cup read was not only fun but surprisingly on point!

Turkish coffee, however, goes beyond Turkey and is its own style and serve. It is popular in many countries, including Greece, Poland, Slovakia and specifically the Balkan regions. The *ibrik* is even recognized on the UNESCO list of Intangible Cultural Heritage!

How to order

If you ever get the chance to visit Turkey, these are some of the most popular Turkish coffee serves:

Sade (sa-deh) – Plain coffee, usually 'single' strength but should be naturally strong.

Az şekerli kahve (ahz sheh-kehr-lee kah-ve) – Coffee with very little sugar.

Orta şekerli kahvesi (ohr-tah sheh-kehr-lee kah-ve-see) – Coffee with a medium scoop of sugar, or one sugar cube.

Çok şekerli kahve (cok sheh-kehr-lee kah-ve) – Coffee with lots of sugar, very sweet.

Duble turk kahvesi (doo-ble turk kah-ve-see) – A very strong 'double' coffee.

Turkish Coffee (*Cezve*)

The unique challenge with Turkish coffee lies in achieving an extremely fine grind, finer than most, almost resembling a powder. To master this brew, it's advisable to use a quality hand grinder or opt for pre-ground Turkish coffee. This recipe makes two cups using a small *ibrik* (Turkish copper coffee pot).

INGREDIENTS

- 20g (¾oz) extra-fine-ground medium-roast coffee
- ½ teaspoon ground cinnamon
- 1 teaspoon sugar (or to taste)
- 200ml (7fl oz) water, at room temperature

METHOD

Place the dry ingredients in the pot and add the water – the ratio is generally 1:10 coffee to water. If the water is at room temperature, it will reduce heating time. Stir the ingredients together and place on a hob over a medium heat. Once it starts to foam and cream, take it off the heat. Do this three times.

After the third heating, pour immediately into 2 espresso cups. Leave to settle for a minute, then enjoy with something sweet like a date or piece of Turkish delight.

Vietnamese Phin Coffee (*Cà phê sữa đá*)

This serve is similar to the Spanish Bombón (see page 118), perfect for those who love a strong, thick and sweet coffee. This coffee is about 2 parts coffee to 1 part condensed milk. It is very easy to make at home and very satisfying. The condensed milk gives the coffee not only a sweetness but a luxurious creamy texture.

The coffee is made with a traditional Vietnamese brewer called a 'phin'. It is a metal vessel that fits on top of a cup. It has a perforated base and two mesh filters that hold the ground coffee, making for a strong, slow brew. If you don't have Robusta beans, use Arabica instead and swap out the condensed milk for a coconut or vegan version if you prefer.

INGREDIENTS

- 20g (¾oz) fine- to medium-ground Vietnamese Robusta coffee
- 200ml (7fl oz) boiling water
- 2–4 tablespoons condensed milk, plus extra to taste (optional)

METHOD

Place the phin directly on top of a jug or glass. Add the ground coffee, then place the gravity press on top. Pour the boiling water into the phin and let the coffee extract and drip into the jug.

Place the condensed milk in a highball glass, add the coffee and use a spoon to stir. Add extra milk to taste.

To make an iced version, cool the phin coffee separately first. Add ice to a tall glass, then the condensed milk. Pour over the cooled coffee, then stir.

Mexican Café de Olla

I've only been to Mexico once, with my mother. I was too young to drink Margaritas (although it didn't stop me from stealing a sip of my mum's) but not too young to taste the sweet coffee.

An 'olla de barro' is a Mexican clay pot. These are traditionally used to cook beans, soups, stews and coffee. This coffee supposedly originated during the Mexican Revolution (1910–17) when it was made by *adelitas*, courageous female soldiers who joined the cause and fought. Infused with cinnamon, cloves and star anise, it is sweetened with a Mexican sugar called *piloncillo*, which is a pure unrefined sugar often shaped like a cone and tasting a little like molasses. If you can't find it, you can replace it with dark soft brown sugar. It's a warming coffee with depth from the spices and the way it's heated. Use a medium to dark roast. Also, note that milk is not traditionally added to this drink as it masks the flavours of the warm spices. Think of this like a coffee version of mulled wine.

INGREDIENTS

- 700ml (1¼ pints) water
- 50g (1¾oz) medium-ground coffee
- 30–50g (1–1¾oz) *piloncillo* or dark soft brown sugar
- 1 cinnamon stick
- 2 cloves
- 1 star anise
- Orange peel twists

METHOD

Place all the ingredients in a saucepan and bring to the boil, then set aside for 6 minutes to steep.

Strain through a sieve lined with a muslin cloth or a paper coffee filter. Serve immediately in small Mexican espresso cups – clay ones if possible. Garnish with orange peel twists from the saucepan.

If you have any coffee left over, allow it to cool and enjoy it over ice.

Spanish Café con Leche

I've been to Spain many times and I love travelling there – the people are fun and there is so much great history and art to see. The coffee scene has grown immensely, especially in the main cities like Barcelona and Madrid, where you have an ever-increasing choice of great speciality cafés. The quintessential Spanish start to the day involves sipping on a *café con leche*, a delightful blend of coffee and heated milk, leaning slightly towards the Latte territory. Just like their Italian counterparts, Spaniards often brew a robust 'espresso' at home, usually using a stovetop moka pot, later infusing it with hot milk. Embracing the trend of smaller coffee vessels, Spain has long steered away from oversized coffee drinks. In the realm of Spanish coffee, size matters – espresso, Cortado, and even the largest – *café con leche* – all come in modest portions.

While the global coffee scene gradually upsizes under the influence of American-style 'grande' servings, Spain stays true to its petite coffee offerings, with espressos and Cortados taking centre stage. As one of the larger servings, *café con leche* is strictly for mornings, very rarely taken after midday, when daintier options like espresso and Cortado are enjoyed.

INGREDIENTS

- 50–60ml (2–2¼fl oz) moka pot coffee
- 100–125ml (3½–4fl oz) milk

METHOD

Make a strong coffee in a moka pot (see page 22). While the coffee is heating, pour the milk into a milk frother or heat in a saucepan.

Once the moka pot top is full, and there is no more coffee bubbling through, take it off the heat and pour into your cup immediately. Add the hot milk to fill the cup.

Spanish Bombón

This originates in Valencia, Spain, and contains 1 part espresso to 1 part condensed milk. I'm lucky as one of my favourite cousins lives there and so does my godson, so I've had an authentic Spanish Bombón in real life, but yours will be just as good if you make it at home. The bitterness of the coffee will help balance the sweetness, but it's an intense drink for those with a sweet tooth. It's not very common to find in cafés, but when I do pop ups, I always like to be prepared for those in the know. Wink wink.

INGREDIENTS

- 30ml (1fl oz) condensed milk
- 1 double shot of espresso
- Frothy milk foam (optional)

METHOD

Place the condensed milk in a clear shot glass and extract the espresso on top. Top with milk foam if you like.

Mazagran

This reminds me of New Zealand, because my home city Dunedin had a really cute coffee roastery/café called Mazagran and growing up I always wondered where the cool name came from! Equally strangely, the first time I had an iteration of the Mazagran coffee was in Barcelona at one of my favourite cafés, Nomad Coffee, who were teaching me how to make their Lemon Coffee Soda, and it blew my mind. This was before the speciality coffee trade was adding flavours into their coffee and it was my first introduction to lemon with coffee. However, Mazagran actually originated in Algeria around 1840, but has been widely claimed, adapted and enjoyed in France, Spain and Austria, as well as Portugal, a place I consider to be my (part-time) home. So in a roundabout way, it still reminds me of home!

The Mazagran, otherwise known as Lemon Coffee, consists of ice, water, espresso and lemon juice. I like to add sparkling water too, which makes it like a coffee lemonade. It is so simple, so fresh and so zingy. Other iterations add sugar, mint, rum and even Cognac.

INGREDIENTS

- Ice cubes
- 1 double shot of espresso
- 15ml (½fl oz) Lemon Syrup (see page 184)
- 100ml (3½fl oz) sparkling water
- Lemon wedges, to garnish

METHOD

Fill a 225ml (8fl oz) glass with ice. Add the espresso and the lemon syrup, then top up with sparkling water. Garnish with a lemon wedge.

Café Cubano

INGREDIENTS

- 1 teaspoon demerara sugar
- 15–20g (½–¾oz) fine-ground coffee

METHOD

Place the sugar on top of your ground coffee in your moka pot or manual espresso machine portafilter, then extract the coffee in the normal way.

This serve originates from Cuba. Here sugar is added to the cup before the coffee is poured. Traditionally, people pour the first few drops from their moka pot in with the sugar, then stir to form a paste (almost like a Dalgona, see page 129). The rest of the coffee is then poured in. But another way to make your coffee this way is to place the demerara sugar with your ground coffee in your moka pot or (gasp) the group handle of your espresso machine first, and tamp down. It's certainly not a traditional method, but a more modern and user-friendly option.

ANZ Flat White

This coffee hails from New Zealand (or possibly Australia) – the origin is a bit hazy and often sparks a friendly debate. I was born in New Zealand, but I did live in Melbourne, Australia, where the coffee is great, so I'll let you decide if there's an unfair bias. Even though it probably should sit alongside the Latte and Cappuccino earlier in the book, I've added the Flat White here because we may never get to the root of its origin. But one thing is sure – it's from the Antipodes!

The idea behind the Flat White, in my mind, was a desire for a coffee with strong espresso flavour, but with added milk that wouldn't compromise the temperature or texture. Cold milk in espresso cools the drink and thins the texture, and adding it to an Americano or Long Black results in a slightly cooled, thin coffee. Enter hot steamed milk, but without too much frothy Latte texture. The drink evolved by adding heated milk to a strong double espresso, with the frothy part held back (often with the back of a spoon), forming a shallow foam, hence the term 'flat'.

Flat Whites used to be served in 225ml (8fl oz) cups, but now are more commonly made in 160–175ml (5½–6fl oz) cups. The milk should be heated to 65–67°C (149–153°F) and be smooth and creamy. The micro-bubbles should be tight and strongly packed together without too much froth on the top – just a creamy layer (see page 27). It's usually smaller, stronger and less milky than a Latte. One thing is sure, however – a proper Flat White should be made with a double espresso, never a single shot.

INGREDIENTS

- 1 double shot of espresso
- 125–150ml (4–5fl oz) heated smooth, velvety milk

METHOD

Extract the espresso into your cup. Heat and texture the milk and pour into the espresso, forming a flat but smooth and creamy head on the coffee.

Fun, one-of-a-kind coffees.

Unicorn
Coffees

6

Dalgona Coffee

Once, having just recently moved countries, I extended an invitation to a new friend to come over, eager to share my love for speciality coffee. He declared his need for an 'extra, extra strong cup of coffee'. It was a chance to dazzle him with the intricacies of the coffee world. I anticipated his reaction to my meticulously crafted, extra-strong V60 concoction that could wake the dead: furrowed brows easing, problems dissipating and a smile stretching across his face. I poured my heart (and an expensive bag of speciality coffee) into making a knockout brew.

As he took the first sip, I held my breath, awaiting the revelation. Instead, he looked me square in the eyes and dropped the bombshell – 'It's not strong enough. Can I just have instant coffee?' My heart cracked a little as he nonchalantly dumped instant coffee straight into my painstakingly brewed V60, no spoon in sight. I couldn't help but chuckle; after all, humour is the best remedy for a broken coffee-loving heart. I guess sometimes there is a call for instant coffee!

This recipe has practically revolutionized the instant coffee market. I admit, I enjoy crafting this beverage. It boasts a fascinating texture and consistently presents an impressive appearance.

INGREDIENTS

- 2 tablespoons instant coffee powder
- 2 tablespoons granulated sugar
- 2 tablespoons hot water
- Ice cubes
- 125ml (4fl oz) milk

METHOD

Place the coffee, sugar and hot water in a small bowl. Using a manual or electric whisk or electric aerowand, whisk the mixture until thick and creamy. If the mixture isn't thickening, add a little more sugar or instant coffee.

Place some ice cubes in a glass and pour over the milk. Spoon the Dalgona mixture on top. This recipe makes a good amount, so feel free to halve the Dalgona ingredients if you prefer.

Iced Boba Coffee

Boba (or bubble) tea has experienced a huge growth in popularity in recent years, and social media has played a large part in spreading the idea of this fun and visually stimulating drink. People love these chewy gelatinous tapioca balls! I like tea, but I love coffee, so here's a simple Iced Boba Coffee recipe to make at home. Only cook the amount of tapioca balls you need, and use them immediately after cooking. They cannot be stored once cooked.

INGREDIENTS

- 30g (1oz) quick-cook tapioca balls
- Chocolate or caramel sauce (optional)
- Ice cubes
- 150–200ml (5–7fl oz) milk
- 1 double shot of espresso
- **Cream,** whipped to soft peaks
- **Hot chocolate powder,** to dust

METHOD

Cook the tapioca balls in boiling water for 5 minutes or follow the packet instructions. Drain and rinse to cool. If you like, drizzle the inside of the glass with chocolate or caramel sauce. Place the tapioca balls in the glass, then add a handful of ice. Pour in the milk, followed by the shot of espresso. Top with whipped cream and dust with chocolate.

Coffee Jelly Whipped Latte

I can see why this has become such a popular coffee, but it does take a little preparation. You'll need to make the coffee jelly first, at least the night before. My version of coffee jelly isn't too solid so it can travel up the straw; it also isn't too sweet as the Dalgona mixture is very sweet already.

INGREDIENTS

- 2 tablespoons instant coffee powder
- 2 tablespoons granulated sugar
- 2 tablespoons hot water
- Ice cubes
- 5–10 small cubes of Coffee Jelly (see page 176)
- 150–200ml (5–7fl oz) chilled milk

METHOD

Place the coffee, sugar and hot water in a bowl. Whisk the mixture until thick and creamy.

Fill a glass with ice and add the jelly. Add the cold milk, leaving about 3cm (1¼ inches) of room at the top of the glass. Spoon on the Dalgona mixture and mix. Enjoy!

Cinnamon Toast Crunch Coffee

There are many different variations of this drink, so feel free to get your creative hat on and add your own touch! The cereal most popularly used in this drink is Cinnamon Toast Crunch, but you can use any cereal you like. However, make sure it has a distinct flavour such as cinnamon or chocolate otherwise it won't really enhance the overall taste of the drink. I've seen this drink made hot or cold. This is my hot version, but if you feel like trying it cold for breakfast, just follow the same recipe but use cold coffee instead and add ice.

INGREDIENTS

- 50g (1¾oz) your favourite breakfast cereal, plus extra to garnish
- 125ml (4fl oz) milk
- 175ml (6fl oz) filter coffee
- ½ teaspoon ground cinnamon
- ¼ teaspoon grated nutmeg
- 2–3 drops of vanilla extract
- **Cream,** whipped to soft peaks
- **Chocolate or caramel sauce or mini marshmallows** (optional)

METHOD

Place the cereal in a bowl and pour over the milk. Stir and leave to soak for 5 minutes.

Brew the coffee, add the cinnamon, nutmeg and vanilla and stir well.

Pour the cereal-soaked milk into the coffee (holding back the cereal). Top with whipped cream and sprinkle some fresh crunchy cereal on top to garnish. Squiggle chocolate or caramel sauce over everything or garnish with mini marshmallows, if you like, and serve.

Espresso Spider Ice Cream Float

An ice cream float is really a drink for kids, but adding coffee makes it adult! Ice cream floats were said to have been created in Philadelphia in 1874 when a café owner ran out of ice for his fruit sodas, and used ice cream instead! These drinks went on to become popular in Britain, Australia and New Zealand as well. The combination of fizzy soda and ice cream creates a sort of web of bubbles, which is why it is also called a 'Spider.' Adding espresso isn't the done thing at a kids' party, but I wanted to try an adult version, and I'm quite happy about it – I hope the parents are too! Feel free to use decaf if the kids feel left out.

INGREDIENTS

- Ice cubes
- 2 scoops of ice cream of your choice
- 1 double shot of espresso
- Cola, raspberry soda or lemonade

METHOD

Place a few cubes of ice in a glass, then add the ice cream. Pour over the coffee, slowly add your soda of choice and watch the fun fizz!

Malibu Dream Coffee

When strawberries are in season, they are so sweet and fragrant. I think this drink would make the perfect morning coffee for Barbie and Ken. Use store-bought or homemade caramel sauce (like the Salted Espresso Caramel on page 187). You can substitute the caramel with white chocolate sauce if you have it and, if strawberries are out of season, use 2 teaspoons of strawberry jam instead.

METHOD

Place the strawberries in a glass, add the salted caramel sauce and mash together. Add some ice cubes, then pour in 150ml (5fl oz) of the milk and the double espresso.

Pour the remaining milk into a jug and use an electric foamer to make it frothy. Pour on top of the drink and top with whipped cream and a sprinkling of hundreds and thousands (sprinkles), if you like.

INGREDIENTS

- 3 large or 6 small strawberries
- 2–3 teaspoons salted caramel sauce
- Ice cubes
- 250ml (9fl oz) chilled milk
- 1 double shot of espresso
- Cream, whipped to soft peaks (optional)
- Hundreds and thousands (sprinkles), to garnish (optional)

Is coffee good for you?

Wellbeing

7

Simply the best

When I proclaimed coffee to be the best thing in the world,
I meant it. There's certainly a strong case for coffee being one
of the best things in the world for our health. It is abundant
in polyphenols, which have antioxidant qualities. These
molecules are found in many plant foods and help to fight off
harmful free radicals linked to such health conditions as cancer
and diabetes. If you've bought or have been gifted this book,
it's likely you're already a fan of the taste of coffee, but few
beverages offer universal accessibility, regular consumption,
joy *and* health benefits! Scientific research is increasingly
revealing the significant health benefits of drinking coffee,
and very few drawbacks.

We all know or have experienced the effects of increased
energy from the caffeine in coffee, which is why many of us
drink it first thing in the morning, or before or after a workout
to keep us going. But studies show that coffee might also lower
the risk of type 2 diabetes and depression, help with weight
management, support brain health, improve liver and heart
health, and increase overall longevity. Not that we needed
an excuse to drink more coffee! Of course there are many
factors to consider, but the research on the health benefits
of coffee is only getting stronger. It's worth noting that there
are antioxidants in instant coffee and they are abundant in
decaffeinated coffee too.

In my opinion, the only caveat to coffee might be the caffeine,
which can affect sleep. And we know that sleep is very
important for our overall growth, regeneration and wellbeing.
An average cup of filter coffee contains 94.8mg of caffeine,
while an average espresso contains 63.6mg. For most people,
the caffeine stays in our bodies for about five hours, so it's
best not to consume strong coffee less than six hours before
bedtime. However, there are now some very well-produced,
high-quality decaffeinated coffees widely available within the
speciality coffee industry. The most important requirement is
that the favourable characteristics of good-quality coffee beans
aren't lost and this is maintained through advanced and usually
natural processing.

There are four main ways to decaffeinate coffee: the ethyl acetate method, methylene chloride method, the Swiss water method and the CO_2 method, which is mostly done with large commercial or supermarket decaf coffees. In my opinion, the best and safest method is the Swiss water method, which regularly ensures the coffee is 99.9 per cent caffeine free. When you're taking anything away from a raw product, it's good to be aware that there might be traces still left behind, but at miniscule levels.

The nature of my barista job meant that, for many years, I was able to have between 5 and 20 espressos a day – when I was constantly sipping and tasting. Of course I didn't always drink the whole cup. But my coffee intake was much higher than it is today and it rarely seemed to affect my sleep too much. As my lifestyle has changed, I now generally have two to three coffees a day and try to consume them before 3pm. However, I do still like to enjoy a cheeky coffee after some meals, and obviously I love my coffee cocktails, which is why decaf coffee is a good option.

As awareness around our health grows, we're presented with numerous studies and strategies to help us make our favourite indulgences healthier or help us explore healthier alternatives. This influx of information reflects our collective desire to balance enjoyment with wellbeing.

There has been a trend towards combining numerous vitamins and supplements with coffee to fuel the hope of maximizing an already amazing drink. While they differ in form (powder or capsules) and strength, I will discuss some of them in this chapter with suggestions on dosage and some classic coffee drinks to aid your healthy lifestyle.

Iced Dirty Matcha

INGREDIENTS

- 1 teaspoon matcha powder
- 50ml (2fl oz) hot water
- Large handful of ice cubes
- 150ml (5fl oz) milk
- 1 double shot of espresso
- Agave syrup or Simple Syrup (see page 184 – optional)

METHOD

Dissolve the matcha powder in the hot water. Once the matcha mixture has cooled, pour it into a glass. Place the ice in the glass and swirl it around a little to chill the matcha.

Hold a teaspoon upside down over the matcha and pour the milk over the back of the spoon and onto the matcha to form a distinct layer. Repeat with the espresso and you should have something that resembles a traffic light! Add some agave or sugar syrup for extra sweetness if needed.

Matcha is a type of green tea, traditionally used in Japanese tea ceremonies. Matcha is created by finely grinding young green tea leaves into a powder and is known for its numerous health benefits, which contribute to its widespread popularity. Combining the benefits of matcha with the antioxidant and energy-boosting qualities of coffee results in a super-powered beverage, also known as a Dirty Matcha. It's worth noting that matcha has more caffeine than regular green tea, but less than coffee, so do be aware of the caffeine levels if it affects you. Otherwise, it's a good dose of healthy antioxidants!

At first I found the two flavours together slightly odd, but I discovered that incorporating milk into a blend of matcha and coffee helps mellow any acidity and diminish the impact of overpowering flavours. You can add some agave or sugar syrup too, to give it some sweetness. It's undeniably a visually appealing drink, which you can easily prepare at home.

Dirty Chai

The term 'dirty' might not sound appealing for a drink, but in the industry it usually indicates that coffee is not the intended ingredient but is included nonetheless. This association initially arose with chai Lattes, as the popularity of chai and tea surged among yoga enthusiasts. Chai itself has a rich history in India going back around 5,000 years. Blending assam black tea with herbs and spices, it was served to the king for Ayurvedic healing.

In modern cafés, the addition of warm frothed milk to chai create a delightful, intriguing drink if done properly. Crafting it with excellent tea, herbs, spices and perfectly textured milk resulted in one of the most memorable drinks I used to make years ago in a Melbourne café. There was something ritualistic about it. As demand grew, it found a spot on the menu and customers – almost conspiratorially – began asking to add espresso for that needed caffeine kick, whispering behind their hand as if sharing a cheeky secret, acknowledging it didn't quite align with the serene, holistic intention traditionally associated with chai. Hence the tongue-in-cheek moniker 'Dirty Chai'.

Prana Chai is a good, widely available brand of ready-made (sticky) chai, but if you just want the flavour, use 30–50ml (1–2fl oz) of shop-bought chai tea syrup instead. Just add it directly to the glass with the espresso and pour the milk on top. If using chai powder, dissolve it in 30ml (1fl oz) of hot water or in the freshly brewed espresso, then add the hot milk.

INGREDIENTS

- 2 teaspoons chai tea mix
- 30–50ml (1–2fl oz) boiling water
- Sugar or honey (optional)
- 200ml (7fl oz) heated textured milk
- 1 double or single shot of espresso

METHOD

Add the chai tea mix to the boiling water in a tea pot and sweeten with sugar or honey if you like. Leave it to steep for a couple of minutes.

Heat the milk, pour it into the chai liquid and stir. Extract the espresso into a cup or glass and then, using a sieve, pour the milky chai in with the espresso.

Iced Dirty Chai

METHOD

Using the same ingredients as above, mix the espresso and brewed and strained chai tea together in a glass. Add ice, and then cold milk. Dust with ground cinnamon or other spices.

Coffee Supplements

Here is a list of possible supplements you can add to your morning coffee to increase its health benefits even further.

MCT oil

This supplement contains medium-chain triglycerides, which are saturated fatty acids (similar to coconut oil) that break down quickly and are easily absorbed. It is said to aid weight loss and improve energy levels. People embracing a ketogenic diet often blend MCT oil into their coffee to help maintain a steadier caffeine effect and to keep hunger at bay, because the oil is processed into ketones, which serve as a sustained energy source.

If you are new to MCT oil, start by adding just 1–1½ teaspoons to your coffee, gradually working up to 1–2 tablespoons. Some people blend in ghee, grass-fed butter or coconut oil, but I prefer the more neutral taste of MCT oil, although high-quality MCT oil is not cheap. If you need more information, Dave Aspery is a well-known biohacker and writes extensively on his 'bulletproof' coffees.

Mushroom coffee

Mushrooms have also gained much attention for their medicinal properties. Traditional Chinese Medicine has been using them for centuries, and now you can have mushrooms in your coffee! No, they're not bobbing up and down, they are dried and ground very finely into a powder. The mushrooms usually used in coffee are Chaga, Turkey's tail, Lion's mane, Reishi and Cordyceps. Their health benefits are said to include improved immunity, lower cortisol levels to help manage stress, lower blood cholesterol to reduce the risk of heart disease and reducing inflammation. However, there is no substantial scientific evidence as yet to certify these claims. I'm a supporter of mushrooms generally, in both food and for medicinal purposes. I've seen some amazing results in people who use mushrooms for medicinal purposes. Numerous brands worldwide offer mushroom coffee and, like anything, it takes consistent use to gain potential benefits.

Mushrooms

Collagen powder

Honey

Matcha

Chai spices

Cinnamon

MCT oil

Cardamom

Turmeric

Collagen powder

Collagen is a crucial protein abundant in our bodies, supporting the functions of bones, skin, muscles, tendons and cartilage. As we age, our ability to produce collagen diminishes, affecting regeneration. It's vital to incorporate collagen-boosting vitamins and minerals into our diet to maintain strength. Personally, I take collagen supplements and consume powdered bone broth when I'm pressed for time. However, some people enjoy incorporating neutral or flavoured collagen protein powders into their coffee. The recommended amount is around 20g (¾oz) per cup, but it's essential to follow the product's instructions. Blending it with milk and creating foam offers an efficient and pleasant way to consume a host of goodness.

Turmeric & maca

Turmeric is a wonderful spice that's easily added to food and is very popular in Lattes. It is thought to have many possible benefits in the treatment of inflammation, arthritis and even anxiety. Many cafés offer turmeric Lattes. It's as simple as mixing ½-1 teaspoon of ground turmeric with espresso, then adding milk and possibly some honey.

Pepper contains a compound called piperine, which helps with turmeric absorption, but in my opinion it isn't necessary in your Latte. Generally, building turmeric into your diet is good for overall wellbeing, but people with liver or gallbladder issues should refrain.

Research has found that maca can improve some aspects of sexual health, fertility, menopause symptoms and sperm quality and can help lift your mood. I find it to have quite a strong taste and gritty texture. It needs some sweetness, so when you're adding it to espresso, you may need to add honey or sugar too. I would use 1-1½ teaspoons of maca in a Latte. It might be better added to food, like my Espresso Energy Balls on page 159 - try adding 1 teaspoon of it to the mixture if you want to try it.

Please note, individual responses vary so consult your healthcare professional before taking any of these substances for health reasons.

Banana Espresso Smoothie

INGREDIENTS

- 1 small banana
- 1 small handful of blueberries
- 6 ice cubes
- 2 tablespoons natural yogurt
- 1 double shot of espresso
- 1 teaspoon honey (or more, to taste)
- 1 tablespoon peanut butter
- ½ teaspoon ground cinnamon, plus extra for dusting
- 100ml (3½fl oz) milk

METHOD

Place all the ingredients in a blender and blend well. Pour into a large glass or two small glasses – this makes about 450ml (16fl oz). Dust with a little cinnamon and enjoy.

If you prefer a thicker smoothie, add more ice to the blender.

Like most people, once I decide to go for something, I really just dive in. I learned a lot during the start of my health and fitness journey, but most importantly the lessons around nutrition and habits have become integral to my life today. Coffee has always been important and enjoyable to me, but it can also be a useful tool for energy.

Waking up at 4:30am became the new norm, allowing me to prep my food for the day and squeeze in intense workouts before a bustling day at the café and evenings dedicated to my business. Time became a precious commodity and smoothies became my go-to solution – quick, nutritious and satisfying. A good smoothie wasn't just a drink, it was an efficient way of staying nourished and energized. Plus, the flexibility allowed me to experiment, adding espresso for an extra kick and making it a delightful and essential part of my routine.

I don't often get up at 4.30am these days unless it's for a flight, but a smoothie is a good vehicle for adding some of the supplements I mention on the previous pages if you find the flavour in coffee alone too overwhelming. Coffee goes well with the banana and yogurt in this recipe, with a little honey to sweeten it up. Have fun experimenting, but here is my go-to smoothie, with added espresso of course! To make this vegan, use vegan yogurt, plant-based milk and agave syrup instead of honey.

Coffee for breakfast, lunch and dinner.

Food

8

Coffee: more than a drink

When I first started blogging on The Girl in the Cafe,
I embarked on a web series, based on a set of interviews
filmed in an award-winning café I managed in London.
My guests were a selection of incredible customers I had met
and made coffee for over the years, who had become good
friends of mine. They were people who were very successful
and had an ethos that aligned with mine, like a BAFTA
award-winning war journalist, a famous actress, a drummer
and a film director, to name a few. To inspire people and
show the essence of human potential, I wanted to share their
stories of triumph and tribulation, then surprise them at
the end by getting them to make me (their barista) a coffee!
It was both hilarious and a moving and insightful example
of vulnerability. One conversation in particular was with a
top Japanese chef in London, Junya Yamasaki. Listening to
him talk about 'nose-to-tail' cooking inspired me to think
about how we eat, how we cook and how we live. At the
time, there were new organic farmers' markets popping
up near my flat, and I was planting my first 'proper' garden,
which started my journey into trying new things with food.

I had been interested in cooking with coffee for a while, but
no one was really doing it, so there weren't many references
to guide me. And back then I considered myself more of
a 'purist' coffee person, so the thought that coffee is only
for drinking, and nothing should really be added to it, was
etched into my brain. But what if I flipped the narrative and
added coffee to something else? I'm glad I did because it's
this thinking that has opened up doors and a more varied
and open-minded way of living for me.

Coffee is very useful in bringing out the flavours in food –
not just your baking, but slow-cooked foods like homemade
baked beans or a stew, for example. I thought that coffee
would add an unpleasant gritty texture when cooked or baked
with, but it dissolves and gives dishes a really interesting
depth. It's also a great way to use up slightly aging coffee that
you don't want to waste and throw away, but don't necessarily
want to drink either. Throw it in your food and eat it!

For dishes like slow-roasted meats or homemade baked beans, stick to your favourite recipes but add between 1 teaspoon and 1 tablespoon of finely ground coffee so that it absorbs well. Treat it as a seasoning, like salt.

This chapter is mainly, though, my favourite quintessential coffee desserts, which are simply the best because coffee always balances sweetness. They are perfect any time you want to celebrate, indulge, impress or share your love of coffee, in a less traditional way than just as a drink. I've included a couple of savoury recipes too, for you to try and experiment with yourself, if you dare! It's exciting that we can use coffee for more than just drinking.

Coffee Pancakes with Espresso Butter

INGREDIENTS

For the espresso butter

- 1 double shot of espresso
- ½ teaspoon instant coffee powder
- 100–125g (3½–4½oz) softened butter
- 2–3 tablespoons icing sugar

For the coffee pancakes

- 150g (5½oz) plain flour
- ½ teaspoon bicarbonate of soda
- 1½ teaspoons baking powder
- ½ teaspoon salt
- 2 tablespoons sugar (add more if you like it sweeter but you can also add maple syrup after)
- 200ml (7fl oz) buttermilk, or 175ml (6fl oz) milk mixed with 2 tablespoons lemon juice
- 1 egg
- 1 tablespoon melted butter, plus extra for frying
- 1 teaspoon Coffee Extract (see page 185 – optional)
- 1 double shot of espresso
- Bacon, maple syrup and fresh fruit, to serve (optional)

There's nothing better than a pancake treat on a weekend morning. Generally I like to do Sundays with delicious fluffy pancakes and a mild black filter coffee or a Flat White. There's a plethora of toppings you can add as well as the espresso butter, from maple syrup to bacon, blueberries, bananas and Nutella.

You can also enjoy the espresso butter on a slice of banana bread with a sprinkle of flaked salt (so good) or on an un-iced slice of coffee cake (see page 167).

METHOD

For the espresso butter, extract the espresso into a cup, stir in the instant coffee and allow to cool. Place all the ingredients in a food processor or blender and mix on high until it is all emulsified and combined. Place in an airtight container with a piece of greaseproof paper on top to seal it completely. This recipe yields 150g (5½oz) and any leftovers can be stored in an airtight container in the refrigerator for several weeks.

For the pancakes, mix the dry ingredients together in a bowl. Place all the remaining ingredients in a jug and beat with a fork to combine. Pour the wet ingredients into the bowl with the dry ingredients and whisk until the mixture is smooth.

Add some butter to a nonstick frying pan on a medium heat, then add a ladle of the mixture. When you start to see bubbles form evenly on the surface of the pancake, flip it over. Once evenly browned on both sides, the pancake is ready to plate up. Repeat with the rest of the mixture. It should make 5–6 large pancakes.

Serve with the espresso butter, and maybe some bacon, maple syrup and fresh fruit.

Espresso Energy Balls

I can't believe I'm sharing this recipe. These were so popular at my pop-ups, other cafés started ordering them from me! Despite constant requests for my secret recipe, I kept it under wraps... until now. You're welcome!

These make the perfect healthy snack. They are gluten free, vegan and use all natural ingredients (with no salt or sugar). Organic ingredients are best too.

Store any leftovers in an airtight container for up to two weeks.

INGREDIENTS

- 2 double shots of espresso or strong filter coffee
- 1 tablespoon raw cacao nibs
- 175g (6oz) pitted dates
- 125g (4½oz) cashew nuts
- 1 teaspoon vanilla extract or ½ vanilla pod soaked in espresso
- 1 tablespoon ground cinnamon
- 1 heaped teaspoon coconut oil
- Desiccated coconut, to coat

METHOD

Blend all the ingredients together in a food processor until combined. If the mixture seems a little soft, add more cashews or coconut oil (this will help them set once cold). Use a teaspoon to form the mixture into 12-14 balls weighing about 20g (¾oz) each. Roll the balls in desiccated coconut to coat them all over, then serve.

Latte Ganache Balls

INGREDIENTS

- 200g (7oz) white chocolate
- 2 teaspoons instant coffee powder, plus extra to coat
- 1 double shot of espresso
- 30ml (1fl oz) double cream
- Pinch of salt
- Cocoa powder, to coat

METHOD

Melt the chocolate in a heatproof bowl over a saucepan of gently simmering water. Dissolve the instant coffee in the espresso, then add to the chocolate with the cream and salt. Once combined and smooth, pour into an airtight container and refrigerate to chill. Once cold, use a teaspoon to form the mixture into 12-14 balls.

Crush a little more instant coffee with the back of a spoon until really fine, then add an equal quantity of cocoa powder and mix well. Roll the balls in this mixture to coat them all over. Store any leftovers in an airtight container for up to two weeks.

Steak with a Dry Coffee Rub ①

This has been such a game changer for me. It is delicious and also acts as a meat tenderizer. I like to cook these steaks in a hot griddle pan, but this is a fantastic recipe for the barbecue too.

INGREDIENTS

- 2 steaks, about 2.5–4cm (1–1½ inches) thick
- Vegetable oil, for rubbing
- Salt
- 2 tablespoons fine-ground coffee
- 1 teaspoon chilli powder
- 1 teaspoon ground cumin
- 1 teaspoon ground coriander
- ½ teaspoon dried mixed herbs

METHOD

Rub the steaks with oil, then lightly season with salt.

Place the coffee, spices and herbs on a plate and mix well. Press the steaks into the coffee mixture, making sure it sticks to all sides. Leave to rest for 30 minutes.

Heat a griddle pan over a high heat until hot. Place the steaks in the dry pan and press flat; they should make a sizzling sound. Cook to your liking. I use the 12345 method for cooking steak:

- 1 minute each side for Blue to Rare
- 1–2 minutes each side for Rare
- 2–3 minutes each side for Medium-rare
- 3–4 minutes each side for Medium
- 4–5 minutes each side for Medium-well done
- 5 minutes each side for Well done

Serve with your choice of sides, such as fries or a green salad with Olive Oil Espresso Vinaigrette (see page 185).

Coffee Sauce for Beef ②

Inspired by one of my favourite spots in Lisbon – a hidden gem where locals gather, laugh and connect over food – this recipe holds a special place in my heart. The old-school taberna, complete with an ageless stainless steel bar, is my go-to spot where I enjoy a solo date-night meal and a beer, or as the locals call it, 'imperial'. The patient and longstanding waitstaff, who have come to know me over the years, endure my attempts at Portuguese as I order the same thing every time to perfect my dash of Portuguese authenticity.

On one occasion, I brought along an American friend. Curious to try something new, I perused the menu and discovered a dish called *bife a café* – beef with coffee sauce. Intrigued, as I'd never heard of this, I decided to step out of my routine. The waiter assured me it's a traditional Portuguese dish and described the sauce – coffee, cream and mustard. Served with medium-rare beef, fries and rice, it was surprisingly delicious and a whole new experience. The coffee flavour really came through strongly, which surprised me, and it combined beautifully with the cream. The waiter revealed the secret: two espressos in the sauce.

Eager to recreate it but with a touch more acidity, and maybe slightly less coffee, I'm sharing this adaptation. It's like a creamy mushroom or peppercorn sauce (but without the mushrooms or peppercorns) and enhances the beef's flavour. I prefer using French wholegrain mustard, but Dijon will work too. The sauce is quite thick and the coffee flavour shouldn't be overpowering. Enjoy this unusual but flavourful journey!

You can serve this sauce with field mushrooms or cauliflower steaks for a vegetarian option.

INGREDIENTS

- 1 double shot of espresso
- 150ml (5fl oz) double cream
- ½ teaspoon wholegrain mustard
- ½ teaspoon salt
- 2 tablespoons lemon juice
- 1 small garlic clove, crushed
- 1 bay leaf
- ½ teaspoon brown sugar, plus extra to taste (optional)
- 1 dried or fresh chilli (optional)
- Splash of bourbon (optional)

METHOD

Place all the ingredients in a saucepan over a medium heat and bring up to a simmer, stirring. Let the sauce simmer for 10 minutes to reduce and thicken. Depending on the strength of your espresso, you can add an extra ½ teaspoon of brown sugar, to taste.

Grill your steak of choice and serve the sauce on the side.

(2) Coffee Sauce
for Beef

Olive Oil Espresso Vinaigrette
(see page 185)

① Steak with a Dry Coffee Rub

Flat White Cookies

Blurring the line between biscuit and cookie, these bakes have a subtle sweetness that makes them irresistibly moreish. The white chocolate atop a rich coffee base, crowned with a smooth milk finish, transforms these Flat Whites into a visual and tasty masterpiece - a cute and delectable pairing for your coffee moments! These are ideal if you have been making Vietnamese coffee (see page 114) and have leftover condensed milk.

INGREDIENTS

- 125g (4½oz) softened butter
- 70g (2½oz) soft brown sugar
- 2 tablespoons condensed milk (optional)
- 1 egg
- 2 tablespoons instant coffee powder, dissolved in 1 tablespoon hot water
- 175g (6oz) plain flour
- 1 teaspoon baking powder
- 1 teaspoon vanilla extract or Coffee Extract (see page 185)
- 70–100g (2½–3½oz) white chocolate
- Chopped dark chocolate or fresh ground coffee, for sprinkling

METHOD

Place the butter and sugar in a mixing bowl and cream together until smooth and pale. Add the condensed milk (if using), egg and dissolved instant coffee and mix again until smooth. Add the flour, baking powder and extract and mix to combine all the ingredients well. You should have a soft brown dough mixture. If it is quite soft, wrap in clingfilm and chill in the refrigerator for 30-60 minutes.

Preheat the oven to 180°C (350°F), Gas Mark 4, and line a baking tray with greaseproof paper. Roll the mixture into 16 balls, flatten slightly and arrange, well spaced, on the baking tray. Bake the cookies for 15-18 minutes, or until golden around the edges. Leave to cool completely on a wire rack.

Melt the white chocolate in a heatproof bowl over a saucepan of gently simmering water. Dip the top of each cookie into the white chocolate and sprinkle the chocolate or fresh ground coffee on top.

Coffee Cake

I am a fan of moist, soft cakes rather than more solid cakes. This one is such a great cake – guaranteed moist and subtle every time. It's also very mess-free and doesn't require an electric beater. It's a great option for that last-minute dinner party or gathering and the mixture can be used to make cupcakes if you prefer. It can be eaten on its own or iced with any of the icings on pages 186–7 – Coffee Buttercream, Coffee Cream Cheese Icing or Coffee Ganache Icing. It's important to ice it with a coffee icing as that brings out the coffee flavour.

To make it vegan, replace the milk with oat milk, and replace the eggs with 2 tablespoons of chia seeds soaked in 6 tablespoons of water for 10 minutes, then stirred until they form a gelatinous texture.

INGREDIENTS

- 150g (5½oz) plain flour
- 100g (3½oz) granulated sugar
- 1 teaspoon bicarbonate of soda
- ½ teaspoon baking powder
- ½ teaspoon salt
- 1 heaped teaspoon cocoa powder
- 1 egg, plus 1 yolk
- 125ml (4fl oz) vegetable oil or light olive oil
- 125ml (4fl oz) buttermilk, or 100ml (3½fl oz) milk mixed with 1 tablespoon lemon juice
- 1 teaspoon Coffee Extract (see page 185)
- 2 teaspoons instant coffee powder, dissolved in 2 double shots of espresso

METHOD

Preheat the oven to 180°C (350°F), Gas Mark 4, and grease and line a 22cm (8½ inch) Bundt tin (though any similar-volume cake tin will work too).

Place all the dry ingredients in a mixing bowl. Add all the wet ingredients and mix using a wooden spoon or hand whisk. It will turn a beautiful caramel-coffee colour. This is quite a wet mixture, so don't fret. Pour into the lined tin and bake for 30–40 minutes or until a skewer inserted into the cake comes out clean. If you leave the cake in for slightly longer, the outside will be slightly harder, but it will still be moist. Turn out onto a wire rack to cool.

Coffee Cream Panna Cotta

INGREDIENTS

- 300ml (10fl oz) double cream
- 2 tablespoons sugar
- 4 tablespoons honey
- 1 double shot of espresso
- 50ml (2fl oz) coffee liqueur
- 12g (scant ½oz) powdered gelatine, dissolved in 3 tablespoons cold water
- Coffee beans, ground coffee or finely grated lemon zest, to garnish

METHOD

Place the cream in a saucepan with the sugar and honey and heat gently to dissolve. Add the espresso, coffee liqueur and dissolved gelatine and bring up to a simmer, stirring. Strain the mixture, divide between 6 small ramekins and put to one side to set.

Using a rubber spatula to help, loosen the panna cottas around the edges, then turn them out onto serving plates. Garnish with coffee beans or freshly ground coffee, or lemon zest to give them a touch of aromatic acidity.

As a variation, you could add ½ teaspoon of finely grated lemon zest to the cream mixture. For a vegetarian alternative, use agar-agar or Vege-Gel instead of gelatine.

Coffee Shortbread

INGREDIENTS

- 200g (7oz) softened butter
- 100g (3½oz) icing sugar
- 125g (4½oz) cornflour
- 175g (6oz) plain flour
- ½ teaspoon salt
- 2 teaspoons fine-ground coffee

METHOD

Put the butter in a bowl, then, using a sieve, add the icing sugar, cornflour, flour and salt. Add the coffee. Rub the mixture together with your fingertips until it forms breadcrumbs. Knead with your hands for about 5 minutes, until there is an even distribution of coffee flecks. Wrap the dough in clingfilm and shape to form an even cylinder, either round or rectangular in cross-section, depending on your desired biscuit shape. Wrap tightly and chill in the refrigerator until firm.

Preheat the oven to 140°C (275°F), Gas Mark 1. Line a baking tray with greaseproof paper. Slice the dough with a sharp knife into 20 biscuits about 2.5cm (1 inch) thick (they will spread a little in the oven) and arrange on the baking tray. Poke some holes in the biscuits with a fork if you like, then bake for 30–40 minutes until golden. Cool on a wire rack.

Tiramisu

Over time, like many chefs and cooks, I've crafted my own version of this delightful dessert – a failproof combination of mascarpone custard and drunken coffee-infused sponge biscuit fingers, all topped with a thick layer of cocoa powder. It's a recipe that never fails to delight any crowd and quite literally translates from the Italian as 'pick me up'. Even non-coffee drinkers can't help but love this one.

There are various theories as to the origin of tiramisu, which is believed to have emerged in the 1960s or 1970s. While some attribute its creation to Turin or Tuscany, many point to Treviso, near Venice – but one thing is certain: it's undeniably Italian! Tiramisu gained popularity in the UK when Nigella Lawson likened it to the Black Forest gâteau of the 1990s.

This recipe can be made with or without pasteurizing the egg yolks. Try to use good-quality eggs. If you want to omit egg altogether, that is possible too. The mascarpone cream will be denser and less aerated but it will still look and taste great. Don't be afraid of going strong on the coffee and liqueur, and try adding the finely grated zest of an orange to the mascarpone mixture at Christmas time. Enjoy this one; you'll feel like a winner.

INGREDIENTS

- 4 eggs, separated
- 125g (4½oz) sugar
- 250g (9oz) mascarpone, at room temperature
- 200ml (7fl oz) double cream
- 200ml (7fl oz) strong filter coffee or espresso
- 30ml (1fl oz) dark spiced rum, madeira or Grand Marnier
- 50ml (2fl oz) coffee liqueur
- 24–30 lady finger biscuits
- 5 teaspoons cocoa powder

METHOD

Whisk the egg yolks and sugar until light and fluffy. If you wish, pasteurize the mixture by placing it in a heatproof bowl over a saucepan of gently simmering water until it reaches 72°C (162°F), then rapidly cool it down in an ice bath.

Beat the mascarpone into the egg yolk mixture. Whip the cream to firm peaks and gently fold it into the mascarpone. Whisk the egg whites separately until they form soft peaks, then gently fold them in too.

Pour the coffee into a shallow dish with the alcohol. Dip each side of the lady finger biscuits into the coffee until just wet, then arrange half of them in a layer in the base of a 23cm (9 inch) serving dish. Be sure not to oversaturate the lady fingers.

Spread half the mascarpone mixture on top of the lady fingers and dust heavily with cocoa. Arrange the remaining dipped lady fingers on top, then add the remaining mascarpone mixture. Dust heavily with cocoa powder again to fully cover the top.

Espresso Martini Meringues

These are the perfect addition to your dinner party or special occasion. Drizzles of vodka syrup takes them to a new level.

INGREDIENTS

- 4 egg whites
- ¼ teaspoon cream of tartar
- 250g (9oz) caster sugar
- 1–2 tablespoons instant coffee powder
- 2 teaspoons cornflour
- 1 teaspoon white vinegar (optional)
- Fresh blueberries or other fruit, to serve
- Grated chocolate, for sprinkling

For the coffee vodka syrup

- 125ml (4fl oz) espresso
- 100g (3½oz) dark soft brown sugar
- 2½ teaspoons arrowroot
- 3–4 tablespoons vodka

For the coffee liqueur cream

- 300ml (10fl oz) extra thick double cream
- 50ml (2fl oz) coffee liqueur
- 1 tablespoon instant coffee (optional)

METHOD

Preheat the oven to 120°C (250°F), Gas Mark ½, and line a baking tray with greaseproof paper.

In a clean, dry bowl, beat the egg whites with the cream of tartar until they form soft, fluffy peaks. Slowly add the sugar, a tablespoon at a time, and continue beating until glossy. Grind the instant coffee to a finer powder using a pestle and mortar or the back of a spoon. Add the coffee to the meringue mixture gradually, along with the cornflour (and the vinegar, too, if you want to make the meringues fluffier) and keep beating until you cannot feel any sugar granules between your fingers. The mixture should look light brown and glossy.

Scoop the mixture onto the lined tray in 8 separate mounds and make an indent in the top of each. Bake for 1¼ hours, then turn off the oven and leave the meringues to cool naturally inside.

For the syrup, heat the coffee and sugar in a small saucepan over a medium heat until simmering. Mix the arrowroot with 2 tablespoons of the vodka until combined. Add this mixture to the coffee and heat until you see it thickening up. Take off the heat and set aside to cool.

When the syrup has cooled, if it is too thick, add another 1–2 tablespoons of vodka to loosen the mixture. If it is not thick enough, mix another ½ teaspoon of arrowroot with a little more vodka, then add to the coffee syrup and heat again to thicken.

To make the coffee liqueur cream, whisk the cream and instant coffee (if using) to soft peaks, then slowly fold in the coffee liqueur with a spatula.

When the meringues and syrup have cooled, dollop the coffee liqueur cream on the meringues, add some fruit and pour the vodka syrup over the top. Sprinkle with grated chocolate.

Mocha Mug Brownie

This is so quick, simple and delicious, especially if you have a microwave – though it's great in the oven too, it just takes a few minutes longer. It's a strong chocolate hit whether you're eating on your own, want a cheeky indulgence after dinner with your loved ones while watching your favourite TV show, or even as a fun treat to make with the kids. It's as easy as throwing all the ingredients into a coffee mug and enjoying the hot chocolatey fudgy goodness in just a few minutes. The coffee really brings out an intense chocolate flavour. Remember, you can use decaf coffee too!

Use brown sugar or less sugar if you don't like your brownie too sweet. If you don't have any espresso, dissolve 1 teaspoon of instant coffee powder in 2 tablespoons of hot water. This is also great topped with a store-bought ice cream mochi.

INGREDIENTS

- 30g (1oz) cocoa powder, plus extra for dusting
- 30g (1oz) plain flour
- 2 tablespoons sugar
- 30ml (1fl oz) vegetable oil or butter
- 2 tablespoons strong espresso
- 1 tablespoon chopped dark chocolate
- 1 scoop of ice cream of your choice or whipped cream, to serve

METHOD

Mix all the ingredients together in a mug and microwave for 1 minute. If the brownie is not quite cooked in the middle, microwave for a further 10-20 seconds. Alternatively, bake in a fan oven at 180°C (350°F), Gas Mark 4, for 12-15 minutes. Once hot, the brownie should be melted and gooey.

Press a small dent in the middle of the brownie with a spoon and top with a scoop of ice cream or whipped cream, dust with cocoa powder and enjoy with an espresso or Iced Latte (see page 55). Be careful though, the brownie is hot!

Coffee Jelly ①

Some people love jelly, some people hate it. I'm on the side of 'depends on what we're eating and how we're eating it'. You don't often see coffee jelly on a menu, or even at house parties, so this is going to be one that is not only edgy and cool, but has a rightful place on the table. Use agar-agar powder or Vege-Gel for a vegan alternative, and double the gelatine or firming agent if you want to set the jelly in silicone moulds. Add the instant coffee if you want a stronger flavour.

INGREDIENTS

- 12g (scant ½oz) powdered gelatine, dissolved in 3 tablespoons cold water
- 250–300ml (9–10fl oz) strong filter coffee
- 1½ tablespoons sugar
- 1–2 teaspoons instant coffee powder (optional)

METHOD

Place all the ingredients in a saucepan and heat gently, while whisking continually. Remove from the heat once it starts to boil and all the ingredients have dissolved. Leave to cool for 5–10 minutes.

Pour into a dish or mould and leave to cool completely, then cover and chill in the refrigerator until set. To serve, sit the mould in warm water for 30 seconds, then turn the jelly out on to a plate.

Coffee Jello Shots

These jello shots are fun to have at parties!

INGREDIENTS

- 18g (scant ¾oz) powdered gelatine, dissolved in 4½ tablespoons cold water
- 250ml (9fl oz) strong filter coffee
- 2 tablespoons sugar
- 100ml (3½fl oz) vodka

METHOD

Follow the method in the recipe above and add the vodka when the mixture is cool. Pour into small shot glasses and place in the refrigerator to set.

No Churn Coffee Ice Cream ②

This ice cream can be made with or without coffee syrup swirls on top. If you want the swirls, make the coffee vodka syrup on page 172, but swap the vodka for water (unless you want a boozy punch). Slowly drizzle the cold syrup on top of the ice cream after transferring to a freezer-proof container and, with the back of a spoon, make swirling patterns on the top before freezing.

INGREDIENTS

- 200g (7oz) mascarpone
- 200g (7oz) condensed milk
- 3 tablespoons instant coffee powder
- 50ml (2fl oz) coffee liqueur or water
- 300ml (10fl oz) double cream
- 1 teaspoon Coffee Extract (see page 185)
- Chocolate chunks (optional)

METHOD

In a mixing bowl, beat the mascarpone with the condensed milk using an electric beater to ensure a smooth consistency. Dissolve 1 tablespoon of the instant coffee in the coffee liqueur (or water), then add to the bowl and mix well. Set aside.

In a second mixing bowl, whip the double cream slowly, gradually adding the remaining instant coffee, until you have slightly firm peaks. Aim for a uniform caramel colour.

Gently fold the condensed milk and mascarpone mixture into the whipped cream using a spatula. Be cautious not to overmix. Add the coffee extract and chocolate chunks, if desired, and continue folding until well combined. The mixture should be light and silky.

Transfer the mixture to a freezer-proof container (an old ice cream tub or enamel dish works well) and swirl the syrup on top, if using. Place it in the freezer for at least 4 hours.

Before serving, take it out of the freezer and let it soften in the refrigerator for about 20 minutes. Serve the ice cream with espresso and enjoy!

① Coffee Jelly

Infusions, syrups and icings.

Coffee
Extras

9

Infusions, syrups and icings are important additions to some recipes to enhance the coffee flavour. Here is a selection to accompany some of the recipes in this book, as well as to have on hand for you to add to any others you wish.

Coffee Liqueur

INGREDIENTS
- 100g (3½oz) coffee beans
- 500ml (18fl oz) spiced rum
- 50ml (2fl oz) Simple Syrup or Coffee Syrup (see page 184)

METHOD

Give the coffee beans a slight smash in a pestle and mortar if you like a strong coffee kick, then place in a large jar with the rum. Seal the jar and leave to infuse for 3–7 days (the longer you leave it, the stronger the flavour).

Strain the liquid into a bottle, add half the syrup and shake to mix. Taste the liqueur and add more syrup if you like it sweeter.

There are many different coffee liqueurs, but my favourites are Kahlúa, Tia Maria and Mr Black. They all taste slightly different, but all pack a great punch of coffee and both Tia Maria and Mr Black are vegan. When I'm in Lisbon, however, it's a challenge to find coffee liqueur, certainly one I like, so having a homemade version is a convenient option.

Making your own liqueur does allow you to control the sweetness, and if you prefer things less sweet like me, the end result is delicious. Opt for an easy spiced rum like Captain Morgan. You can throw in a cinnamon stick, ½ a vanilla pod or other spices if you like it spicier, but I keep it simple to let the coffee flavour shine. I use 1 part coffee to 3 or 4 parts rum. Approximate measurements are okay – the more coffee, the stronger the batch.

This can be used to make Espresso Martinis and other drinks, but is great for sipping neat too.

Coffee Vermouth

The Negroni is probably my favourite cocktail. However, it gets even better with a touch of coffee, which adds some depth to the cocktail but remains subtle (see page 81). One of the things about a Negroni is the strength – by infusing the vermouth with the coffee, rather than adding liquid coffee to the drink, you aren't diluting or changing the ratios too much. Ideally, you would use a slow coffee dripper specifically made for cold brew. However, most people don't have one, and using a pourover coffee filter or simply immersing the coffee in a jar of vermouth is fine.

INGREDIENTS

- 60g (2¼oz) medium- or fine-ground coffee
- 300ml (10fl oz) sweet vermouth

METHOD

Option 1: Line a pourover cone with a paper filter and add the ground coffee. Pour over some of the vermouth, making sure all the coffee is saturated. Give it a gentle stir, then continue to slowly pour in the vermouth, as if you're making a coffee. The vermouth should come out slightly darker.

Option 2: Place the coffee in a large jar with the vermouth and stir gently to make sure all the grounds are saturated. Cover and leave for 2 hours, then strain through a paper coffee filter, a muslin cloth or a paper towel.

Simple Syrup or Coffee Syrup

Traditional simple syrup is made with 1 part sugar to 1 part water. So to make a simple coffee syrup, simply use espresso or filter coffee instead of the water. Espresso will give a stronger flavour. You could also add ground coffee to a simple syrup, then strain afterwards, but it is an extra step.

INGREDIENTS

- 125ml (4fl oz) water, filter coffee or espresso
- 125g (4½oz) granulated sugar
- ½ teaspoon vanilla extract (optional)

METHOD

Place the water or coffee, sugar and vanilla in a saucepan over a medium heat and bring to the boil, stirring, until the sugar has dissolved. Allow to cool, then store in a sealable bottle or jar in the refrigerator for up to 1 month.

To make a lemon syrup (see Mazagran, page 121), use lemon juice instead of water or coffee.

To make a demerara syrup (see Coffee Old Fashioned, page 82), use demerara sugar instead of granulated sugar.

Ginger Syrup

Fresh root ginger results in a syrup with a bit more bite than ground ginger, ideal for flavouring coffee (see Gingerbread Latte, page 100).

INGREDIENTS

- 125g (4½oz) fresh root ginger, sliced with skin on
- 200g (7oz) brown or muscovado sugar
- 200ml (7fl oz) water
- ½ teaspoon ground cinnamon (optional)
- Pinch of grated nutmeg (optional)

METHOD

Place all the ingredients in a saucepan over a medium heat and bring to the boil, stirring, until the sugar has dissolved and the syrup is fragrant and thickened. Leave to cool, then strain out the ginger slice using a sieve. Transfer to a bottle or airtight container and refrigerate for up to 2 weeks.

Coffee Extract

This extract makes a lovely ice cream topping. It can also be used to flavour mascarpone and cream, or to enhance flavouring in cakes. You can omit the sugar if you prefer a more intense coffee flavour.

INGREDIENTS

- 250ml (9fl oz) strong espresso or moka pot coffee
- 1–2 tablespoons sugar
- 2 tablespoons coffee liqueur (optional)

METHOD

Place the coffee in a saucepan and bring to the boil. Boil for 5 minutes to make a reduction. Add the sugar and keep simmering for another 5 minutes, or until reduced and thickened. Mix in the coffee liqueur, if using, and leave to cool. Store in a sealable bottle or container in the refrigerator for up to 1 month.

Olive Oil Espresso Vinaigrette

During a memorable evening in Milan at a restaurant called Taglio (sadly no longer open), my brother and I were treated like royalty by the owner. Amid the feasting and coffee making at my table, another surprising twist awaited me. The seemingly typical bowl of olive oil and balsamic vinegar served to us for dipping the soft sourdough bread in turned out to be a blend of richness and boldness – espresso. A unique take on the traditional Italian flavours, right in the heart of espresso's homeland. Recreating this experience at home is simple: combine high-quality extra virgin olive oil with a shot of espresso, allowing the espresso to settle at the bottom like balsamic vinegar. Add a squeeze of lemon juice if you desire, and dip into this unique, flavourful blend a delicious knob of sourdough bread.

Alternatively, drizzle it on top of your tomatoes and burrata – we were offered that experience too. Adding a few other ingredients creates a simple coffee dressing that will grace any salad, burrata or even grilled vegetables.

INGREDIENTS

- 2 tablespoons espresso
- 4 tablespoons extra virgin olive oil
- ½ teaspoon salt
- 2 tablespoons lemon juice or apple cider vinegar
- ½ teaspoon chilli powder or flakes (optional)
- Grinding of pepper
- 1 teaspoon honey or brown sugar

METHOD

Combine all the ingredients in a small cup or dish and mix well.

Coffee Buttercream

- 1 tablespoon instant coffee powder
- 1 teaspoon boiling water
- 1 teaspoon lemon juice
- 125g (4½oz) icing sugar
- 125g (4½oz) softened butter

METHOD

Mix the coffee, water and lemon juice in a mixing bowl until the coffee has dissolved. Sieve the icing sugar into the bowl and add the butter. Mix with an electric beater or whisk until smooth and creamy.

Coffee Whipped Cream

This is great in a pavlova, on top of meringues or served alongside coffee cake.

INGREDIENTS

- 200ml (7fl oz) double cream
- 1 tablespoon icing sugar
- 1 teaspoon instant coffee powder
- 1 tablespoon coffee liqueur (optional)

METHOD

Whip the cream with the sugar and coffee powder until it forms soft peaks. Whip the cream a bit more to get slightly firmer peaks if you're using the liqueur. Now fold in the liqueur if using.

Coffee Cream Cheese Icing

This should be enough to ice one cake, giving a lovely smooth tan-brown colour. The lemon zest balances out the flavour of the coffee and sugar. If you'd like flecks of coffee in the icing, keep back half the coffee to stir in at the end, after mixing.

INGREDIENTS

- 2 teaspoons instant coffee powder
- 1 teaspoon boiling water
- 30g (1oz) softened butter
- 200g (7oz) cream cheese
- 125g (4½oz) icing sugar
- ½ teaspoon lemon zest

METHOD

Dissolve the coffee in the water in a cup. Using an electric beater or whisk, mix the butter and cream cheese together in a bowl until combined and soft, then fold in the icing sugar, lemon zest and dissolved instant coffee. Make sure to mix well. If you get lumps, scrape the icing through a sieve.

Coffee Ganache Icing

This makes a perfect icing for coffee cake (see page 167).

INGREDIENTS

- 150g (5½oz) white chocolate
- 45ml (1½fl oz) double cream
- Pinch of salt
- 1–2 teaspoons instant coffee powder
- 1 double shot of espresso

METHOD

Melt the chocolate in a heatproof bowl over a saucepan of gently simmering water. Add the remaining ingredients and whisk together until melted and smooth. Remove from the heat and leave to cool a little before pouring over a cake while it is still runny. It will set at room temperature, but it will be quicker in the refrigerator.

Salted Espresso Caramel

Serve with ice cream, use to rim glasses or to add a caramel flavour to cocktails and hot espresso-based drinks. Add 20g (¾oz) of butter with the sugar if you are serving this with ice cream.

INGREDIENTS

- 40g (1½oz) caster sugar
- 20g (¾oz) brown sugar
- 1 tablespoon golden syrup or honey
- 100ml (3½fl oz) double cream
- 1 double shot of espresso
- ¼ teaspoon flaked sea salt

METHOD

Place the sugars and golden syrup or honey in a saucepan over a low heat until the sugar crystals start to dissolve. Add the cream and increase the heat. Simmer and stir for a few minutes, until the caramel becomes shiny and golden. Add the espresso and salt, heat for a couple more minutes, then remove from the heat and allow to cool. Store in the refrigerator for up to 2 weeks.

Index

Acknowledgements

I am so grateful to the remarkable souls who've supported or guided me throughout my life which has helped me create a one-of-a-kind journey full of excitement and discovery – a coffee-journey that's led me right to the pages of this book. A deep heartfelt thank you.

Most honourable mentions: Jennifer at Features UK (my literary and media management agent); the teams and individuals who make coffee greatness possible at Melitta UK, La Marzocco, Ozone Coffee UK, Climpson & Sons, Flat White, Code194.Coffee, Pavilion Bread, AeroPress and Brades Farm Barista Milk – your continued support and effortless collaboration is highly appreciated and invaluable.

Special thanks to the incredible team at Octopus Publishing for their collaborative spirit and unwavering dedication, making this journey truly enjoyable.

To my mentors, friends, and taste testers, who've lent their time, expertise, given urgent feedback, and respectfully told me (on occasion) to possibly lay off the coffee during my inspired midnight recipe sessions... your contributions and insights have been priceless throughout my life and specifically in writing this book. Conroy, Tara, Amy B, Pam and Brian, Chelsea, Lucie, Jade, Tans and Jase, Cameron, Dumo, and my Lisbon and London crew – your talent and friendship mean the world to me.

Thank you so much to the special CC book fam: Jeannie, Yasia, Scarlet, Allison, Jo, Steve, Jake, Morgan, Christina, Max, Olive, Sophie, Vicky (at Fresh Locations), Rosie (at Shag Hair) ... 'NAILED IT!' The next round is on me!

To the entire specialty coffee industry, hardworking baristas, coffee growers, hospitality workers, entrepreneurs and creators, you inspire me daily. To all the readers, coffee lovers and enthusiasts, thank you for welcoming me into your home and hearts. It is my deepest hope that this book brings even more joy and inspiration into your lives.

Coffee, I love you dearly. Yours truly FOREVER,

Celeste xx

Picture Credits